POLITICS and
COMMUNICATION

The Little, Brown Series
in Comparative Politics

Under the Editorship of
GABRIEL A. ALMOND

JAMES S. COLEMAN

LUCIAN W. PYE

AN ANALYTIC STUDY

POLITICS and COMMUNICATION

Richard R. Fagen

Stanford University

Boston
LITTLE, BROWN AND COMPANY

Published simultaneously in Canada
by Little, Brown & Company (Canada) Limited

PRINTED IN THE UNITED STATES OF AMERICA

Foreword

THE Little, Brown Series in Comparative Politics has three main objectives. First, it will meet the need of teachers to deal with both Western and non-Western countries in their introductory course offerings. Second, by following a common approach in analyzing individual political systems, it will make it possible for teachers to compare these countries systematically and cumulatively. And third, it will contribute toward re-establishing the classic relationship between comparative politics and political theory, a relationship which has been neglected in recent decades. In brief, the series seeks to be global in scope, genuinely introductory and comparative in character, and concerned with broadening and deepening our understanding of the nature and variety of political systems.

The series has two parts: the Country Studies and the Analytic Studies. The Country Studies deal with problems and processes deriving from a functional, as compared with a purely structural, approach to the study of political systems. We are gratified that the participants, all mature scholars with original insights, were willing to organize their discussions around a common set of functional topics in the interest of furthering comparisons. At the same time, each author has been urged to adapt the common framework to the special problems of the country he is discussing and to express his own theoretical point of view.

A forthcoming introductory book, *Comparative Politics: A Developmental Approach,* written by Gabriel A. Almond and G. Bingham Powell, provides an analytic supplement to the Country Studies. It also opens our set of Analytic Studies, which will offer basic discussions of such topics as political change in the emerging nations, comparative analyses of interest groups, political socialization, political communication, political culture, and the like. We hope these books will prove to be useful and stimulating supplements to the Country Studies as well as points of departure in more advanced courses.

In *Politics and Communication* Richard R. Fagen presents a systematic discussion of the relationship between communication systems and the operations of different types of political systems. In dealing with such problems as the social, cultural, economic, and historical determinants of communication patterns he suggests new perspectives for viewing basic social and political processes. He also reviews existing knowledge about the influence of communication structures and patterns on the distribution of political beliefs.

In addition to descriptive analysis Fagen turns in his last chapters to some normative issues about adequacy in the performance of political systems, the concepts of political change and development, and the problems of freedom and restraint. In analyzing these basic problems in political theory from the vantage point of communication theory, Fagen makes a significant contribution to the reintegration of normative political theory and contemporary social science.

Gabriel A. Almond
James S. Coleman
Lucian W. Pye

Preface

It is worth stating what this little book is intended to be and
to do. Quite simply, it is an investigation into and an argument in support of the usefulness of a communication approach to the study of comparative politics. Designed as an
introduction to the subject, these are several of its characteristics: The presentation is informal. What we offer is a number
of probes into the subject. Thus, the reader will find more
examples than definitions, more suggestions than hypotheses,
and footnotes that are intended to comprise no more than an
introduction into the literature. Examples incorporated into
the text reflect personal experiences and interests. These examples have been selected because they were familiar or perhaps dramatic, not necessarily because they were the most
representative episodes culled from a large sample. The empirical materials are intended to illustrate and clarify points
made in the analytical narrative, not to prove or disprove the
argument.

In the course of thinking about communication and politics
and putting these ideas down on paper, I have incurred a
special debt to the writings of a number of scholars. Although
this debt is in part acknowledged in the footnotes, my dependence on the work of these men is actually more enduring than
such occasional references would indicate. Thus it seems only
proper to state at the beginning that the work of Almond,
Boulding, Deutsch, Easton, Kuhn, Lasswell, Lerner, Pye, and
Schramm, has over the years sown seeds which have contrib-

uted most significantly to the growth of the hybrid presented
on the following pages. More immediately, Gabriel Almond,
Ole Holsti, Frederick Reis, and Sidney Verba, all of Stanford,
and Lucian Pye of the Massachusetts Institute of Technology
have read and commented on the manuscript. Where my own
pride and prejudice have not prevented, their suggestions have
been incorporated into the text. Certainly I have profited
greatly from their repeated warnings to keep my eyes on the
political system and my feet on the ground. Over the past
several years, I have also learned much — first as student and
then as colleague — from Heinz Eulau and Robert North.
Their imprint on this volume is once removed, however, because they were wise enough to be in Europe when the manuscript was in preparation and thus were spared exposure to
the several drafts.

I am in debt also to Mrs. Sally M. Harms who not only
typed and retyped the manuscript but also remained cheerful
and cooperative when lesser spirits were wrapped in gloom.
My wife and three small daughters have also contributed: The
former because she constructed the index and kept her hands
on the manuscript, and the latter because in general they kept
their hands off.

Table of Contents

POLITICS and
COMMUNICATION

CHAPTER I

Introduction

POLITICS AND COMMUNICATION

FEW AMERICANS over twenty years of age cannot recall with vividness the sequence of events which took place in Dallas on November 22, 1963: President Kennedy riding with his wife and others in a slowly moving motorcade; a number of shots, the President falling to his left onto Mrs. Kennedy's lap; later, confusion and finally the death announcement at Parkland Memorial Hospital; then Mrs. Kennedy, her suit stained with blood, standing with President and Mrs. Johnson in the presidential jet as the inaugural oath is administered. Subsequent images are almost equally vivid: Lee Harvey Oswald clutching his stomach and doubling over as he is shot by Jack Ruby in the basement of the Dallas city jail; the horse-drawn and flag-draped casket moving through the streets of Washington to the sound of drums; the leaders of the world and their representatives in silent assembly at the funeral.

Yet no matter how real and vivid these and other fragments of the drama may seem, it is well to remember that relatively few persons actually witnessed any of the events mentioned, and no single person was direct witness to all of them. The mass media provided the vital link between the actors and us. Whatever reality and coherence the events hold for us derive in part from the manner in which they were *communicated*, the monopoly of attention given to the assassination, the seriousness

1

and solemnity of the treatment. In fact, in a very real sense it can be said that the assassination came to assume full political meaning *only* as it was communicated to increasing numbers of Americans, only as it became *communis,* common. We live in an age when the "death of kings," the traditional subject of classical tragedy, can be brought into tens of millions of homes with dazzling speed and intimacy. As surely as this is the atomic age, it is also the communication age.

Consider a second event, equal in precipitousness to the Kennedy assassination: The Japanese attack on Pearl Harbor. But let us concentrate for a moment not on communication about the event to the public at large, but rather communication to and from special audiences such as military units, the President and Congress, foreign governments, and the news and information services of the world. The number of messages that were generated, transmitted, and received in the first twenty-four hours alone must have been astronomical. Information had to be gathered on the extent and meaning of the attack, military outposts around the world had to be alerted and instructed. Diplomatic centers had to be similarly informed. Massive two-way exchanges took place as information was gathered in the field, collected in decisional centers, action was taken, and then instructions were relayed back to the field. The attack must have been the number one news story in almost every capital of the world, and even in 1941 the networks of men and machinery which existed to bring the story to such far-flung places as Cape Town, Kabul, and Wellington were impressive indeed.

War and the death of kings, two events which from the earliest recorded history of man have loomed large in political life and have thus occasioned a great deal of communication.

But let us not extend too easily in time or in space the political implications of this awesome capacity for communication as it operated to inform the American people and others about the death of the President and the attack on Pearl Harbor. Two cautionary points are in order. First, this capacity does not exist in many parts of the world. We should not have to be reminded that in dozens of nations television is just emerging, radio is in its infancy, and when newspapers operate they speak only to the small fraction of the population that is literate. Second, whatever the national level of development in communication, not only high drama but also some mixture of low comedy, fatuous nonsense, and outright untruth fills the columns, the airwaves, and the television screens. In the United States, and in almost all other parts of the world, the involvement, the scope, and the monopoly of people's attention that characterized communication about the assassination are the very rare exception, not the rule. In more normal times the "average" citizen ingests a mass communication diet of crime, sports, a little political news and opinion, and a rather large helping of entertainment. Thus we stay sporadically in touch with the politically relevant world; now through the rapid and global coverage provided by the mass media and specialized agencies of government using the very latest technological innovations, and in earlier times through the less rapid and certainly less complete system in which the runner or horsemen carried messages from place to place and the priest, the official, or the crier disseminated them to the public. And now as in the past it is difficult to separate the quality and cast of political life from the methods of communication that sustain it.

But behind the changes wrought by technology, organization, and the scale of politics, there is also a certain sameness. Today, as three thousand years ago, the king still counsels with his ministers, peasants still gather in the fields and complain about government, men still meet in the coffee houses to argue about politics, and the citizens still weep in the streets when the royal bier passes. Linked to the communication structures which characterize a society, and in fact inseparable from them, are numerous face-to-face relationships. Some are casual and fleeting, a chance encounter; others are enduring. Much of the political business of the world still is done in such situations, and it would indeed provide a mistaken view of the communication process to concentrate on machines and organizations to the exclusion of the face-to-face groupings which are a prominent feature of all political systems.

What is being pointed out, of course, is that ultimately the communication process as it interests us must focus both on man himself and on the artifacts which man the toolmaker has created to extend his communicatory powers. No matter how a man's words and actions are multiplied and diffused by technology, no matter how impressive the structure of the mass media or the political organizations that he commands, it is still man the symbol producer and manipulator who stands as the one indispensable link in the communication process. The other side of this coin is the more general proposition that it is precisely man's communicatory capacity that makes social life (and therefore political life) as we know it possible. Communication is basic to all social and political activity.

But neither the examples given nor abstractions about the centrality of communication to all political life get us very deeply into the subject matter at hand, so let us begin our investigation with a brief "communications" look at some of the common concerns of students of politics. This will remind us of some of the difficulties in an attempt to relate communication to politics. That is, once we abandon a straight empirical approach to our subject matter, once we admit that it is not just the press and the President, or television and voting, or communication between bureaus in the State Department that we wish to examine, we are in danger of losing our way. It is the purpose of this and the following chapter to set out some guideposts and establish some limits for our inquiry.

As an initial point of reference — since we lack a more explicit framework at this time — it is useful to keep Lasswell's familiar formula in mind. The study of communication, he says, involves finding out "Who Says What, In Which Channel, To Whom, With What Effect." [1] As simple as this paradigm is, it

[1] Harold D. Lasswell, "The Structure and Function of Communication in Society," in Lyman Bryson, ed., *The Communication of Ideas* (New York: Harper & Row, Publishers, 1948), p. 37, punctuation added.

Webster's Third New International Dictionary defines communication as "Intercourse by words, letters, or messages; interchange of thoughts or opinions by conference or other means." Though not very formal, this definition will serve about as well as any other to suggest the meaning in-

continues to direct us toward a host of important political problems. In fact, the most enduring of all concepts in the political lexicon, the concept of power (and/or influence) is inextricably linked to communication. We cannot conceive of the exercise of power by individual A over individual B without some communication from A to B. This communicatory activity may be as direct and open as caveman A's threat to bash caveman B unless the latter hands over his catch. Or the activity may be as indirect and difficult to isolate as the web of messages, perceptions, and expectations which ultimately enables the Prime Minister to convince the leader of the opposition to support him on a crucial issue. But in both cases, when individuals are in a relationship of power or influence, they are also of necessity in communication.

Similarly, when we are dealing with larger aggregates and trying to understand either their internal processes or their relationships with other institutions, we quite easily turn to the study of communication. Ask a question as deceptively simple as, "How did the Congress come to ratify the partial Test Ban Treaty of 1963?" and you can generate a host of subsidiary questions with communication overtones. For instance, how did groups and individuals supporting or opposing the treaty make their positions known to the Congress? What was the patterning and content of bargains, threats, and promises exchanged within Congress itself while the treaty was being debated? How did the mass media report and comment on the issues involved, and how were these messages perceived and acted upon both by decision-makers and by the public at large?

---

tended for "communication" in this book. For more analytical and technical treatments of the concept see Colin Cherry, *On Human Communication* (New York: John Wiley & Sons, 1957), particularly Chapter 1; Karl W. Deutsch, *The Nerves of Government* (New York: The Free Press of Glencoe, Inc., 1963), particularly Chapters Five and Nine; Alfred Kuhn, *The Study of Society* (Homewood, Illinois: Dorsey Press, 1963), particularly Section II. All three of these books should be read in their entirety by anyone seriously interested in politics and communication. See also Edward Sapir, "Communication," *Encyclopaedia of the Social Sciences*, Vol. IV (New York: The Macmillan Company, 1931) for an early but still excellent statement.

The list, of course, could be extended, but many a lengthy dissertation has grown out of an even more limited set of queries than those already mentioned.

Or consider the field of international relations. The exchanges of documents, people, goods, and even violence that take place across national boundaries can almost all be considered as forms of communication. To pick only one possible example, the notion of deterrence is inextricably bound up in communication. When the strategist says, "Defense and retaliatory posture X if employed by country A will deter country B from attacking," he is actually predicting that X communicated by A to B is sufficient to convince the leaders of B that attacking A is too costly. Again, this skeletal formulation masks a variety of derivative communication questions of great complexity and importance.

In another vein, the great controversies involving the citizen's right — or lack of right — to criticize the established order are at heart controversies about communication. Much legal and philosophical argument even to this day focuses on a *normative* version of the Lasswellian formulation: Who *should* be able to say what, in which channels, to whom, for what purposes? The problem is very old, and it is central to the debates about the good society as they have come down to us through the centuries. If we recall Socrates' famous admonition to the jury which had just condemned him to death, we realize that the controversy is as fresh today as it was almost two and a half millennia ago:

> You have brought about my death in the belief that through it you will be delivered from submitting your conduct to criticism; but I say that the result will be just the opposite . . . If you expect to stop denunciation of your wrong way of life by putting people to death, there is something amiss with your reasoning. This way of escape is neither possible nor creditable; the best and easiest way is not to stop the mouths of others, but to make yourselves as good men as you can.[2]

[2] Plato, *The Apology* in *The Last Days of Socrates,* translated by Hugh Tredennick (Baltimore: Penguin Books, Inc., 1959), pp. 73-74.

As long as complex social organization persists, the cluster of problems that we group under the heading of "freedom of expression" will continue to be of political relevance.

The possibility of thinking about so many aspects of political life with communication in mind is both a blessing and a curse. On the credit side, there arises the possibility of imposing conceptual unity on otherwise disparate phenomena. How attractive and useful it would be if we could develop communication models of sufficient scope and power to handle within a common frame of reference the diversity of subjects — both empirical and normative — about which students of politics now worry.[3] But on the debit side, there looms the danger of diffuseness. In the absence of a widely accepted and very general theory of politics based on communication, we have great difficulty in setting any boundaries to what might be called "a communication approach to the study of politics," an approach in which communication as a process is seen as central to an understanding.[4] The dilemma is made graphic if we think for a moment about the bibliographical dimensions of the problem. In a "selected" bibliography appended to a recent work on communication and comparative politics, over two hundred titles are mentioned, drawn from such diverse fields as history, sociology, anthropology, psychology, and journalism in addition to political science.[5] Almost two decades ago, a less selective bibliography easily achieved a length of several thousand entries while the authors with due modesty protested incompleteness.[6] At present, the burgeoning

[3] The most impressive efforts in this direction have been made by Karl Deutsch, *op. cit.*

[4] At this juncture we shall not attempt to clarify the fuzziness associated with the notion of "a communication approach to the study of politics." One of the primary purposes of Chapters III through VIII is to provide just such a clarification. In those chapters we suggest what a general commitment to the study of communication might lead us to look for when examining problems of importance to the student of comparative politics.

[5] Lucian W. Pye, ed., *Communications and Political Development* (Princeton, N.J.: Princeton University Press, 1963).

[6] Bruce Lannes Smith, Harold D. Lasswell, and Ralph D. Casey, *Propaganda, Communication, and Public Opinion* (Princeton, N.J.: Princeton

interest in subjects such as public opinion, political culture, decision making, propaganda, and political socialization — all of which seem inescapably bound up with communication — makes our hypothetical bibliography of works relevant to the "communication approach to politics" seem infinitely elastic.[7]

Thus we begin our investigation faced with three important facts of life. First, communication as a process pervades politics as an activity. Second, even when it is not immediately obvious, we can describe many aspects of political life as types of communication. Third, because of the pervasiveness of the communication process and the elasticity of the conceptual vocabulary of political science, there is an almost limitless literature "of possible relevance" to the study of politics and communication. Nothing we can do or say here will change this basic situation.

We are nevertheless faced with the pragmatic task of select-

University Press, 1946). The volume contains almost 3,000 annotated entries in the bibliographical section. A follow-up work of more limited substantive scope adds another 2,500 titles to the list. See Bruce Lannes Smith and Chitra M. Smith, *International Communication and Political Opinion* (Princeton, N.J.: Princeton University Press, 1956). Over the past decade, of course, many more thousands of "possibly relevant" books and articles have appeared.

[7] Almost any important recent work in political science would qualify for inclusion on such a diffuse listing. Consider the three most recent winners of the annual Woodrow Wilson Foundation Award for "the best [American] book on government, politics or international affairs." In 1962 the award was won by Robert A. Dahl, *Who Governs* (New Haven, Conn.: Yale University Press, 1961). Dahl's book has important sections on communication among leadership groups, between leaders and the public, and between bureaucrats and their clientele. The winner in 1963 was Inis L. Claude, Jr., *Power and International Relations* (New York: Random House, Inc., 1962). His three macroconcepts — balance of power, collective security, world government — all imply certain content and patterns of communication between national actors. Although Claude seldom deals explicitly with communication variables, no one who is seriously interested in international communication would want to overlook his book. In 1964 the award was won by Raymond A. Bauer, Ithiel de Sola Pool, and Lewis Anthony Dexter, *American Business and Public Policy* (New York: Atherton Press, 1964). The first half of this book is, in essence, a communications analysis. The chapters bear titles such as "Public Attitudes on Foreign Trade," "Channels of Information," and "Communicating with Congress."

ing from this empirical, conceptual, and bibliographical cornucopia materials for incorporation into the chapters which follow. How might this be done? What criteria might be used?

One guideline, of course, is readily available: We want to select ideas and materials of immediate relevance to the field of comparative politics as presently constituted. Therefore, topics such as international bargaining and deterrence are automatically excluded. But this is only the grossest sort of limitation. Moreover, we have not yet answered an unstated but prior question: Why bother? Less rudely, what is there about the study of comparative politics which leads us to believe that at this time it would profit by being approached from a communication point of view? It is to this question that we now turn.

COMMUNICATION AND COMPARATIVE POLITICS

Current work in comparative politics reflects the partial confluence of three streams of thought and inquiry. The first two are the theoretical and empirical branches of the "behavioral revolution"; the third is the resurgence of interest in the classical problems of political philosophy.[8] Without reviewing subjects which have been treated in great detail elsewhere, we can nevertheless suggest why the present time seems particularly congenial, conceptually and methodologically, to an assessment of communication as it relates to the study of comparative politics.

To be more specific, out of the welter of theory, research, and polemic in comparative politics, three trends stand out as particularly heartening to those who would use the study of communication as an avenue of approach into the study of the

[8] Readers for whom this cryptic characterization connotes little would do well to consult the following three essays and some of the bibliography cited therein. For an overview of the development of comparative politics as a field, see Harry Eckstein, "A Perspective on Comparative Politics, Past and Present," Part I in Harry Eckstein and David E. Apter, eds., *Comparative Politics* (New York: The Free Press of Glencoe, Inc., 1963). For an analysis of the relationship between theory and behavioral research see David Easton, *A Framework for Political Analysis* (Englewood Cliffs, N.J.: Prentice-Hall, Inc., 1965), Chapter I. For one interpretation of the relationship between comparative politics and classical political thought see David E. Apter, "Past Influences and Future Development," Part X in Eckstein and Apter, *op. cit.*

polity. These trends are directly derivative of the three more general streams of thought and inquiry mentioned in the previous paragraph.

1. *Cybernetics, Systems Theory, and Derivative Models of the Polity.* The impact of cybernetics — the science of communication and control — on comparative politics has been more thoroughgoing than a casual reading of the literature might indicate. With the exception of the work of Deutsch and a few others, however, this impact has not been direct.[9] Rather, cybernetics has filtered down — and in the process has been partially transmuted — through what has come to be called the systems approach to the study of politics.

In order to get some feeling for the relationship between cybernetic ideas and the systems approach, consider the following formulation by Easton:

> Systems analysis as conceived here will be built upon the following general premises. Only the first two of these need it share with other modes of analysis that revolve around the concept "system" as a primary axis.
>
> 1. *System.* It is useful to view political life as a system of behavior.
>
> 2. *Environment.* A system is distinguishable from the environment in which it exists and open to influences from it.
>
> 3. *Response.* Variations in the structures and processes within a system may usefully be interpreted as constructive or positive efforts by members of a system to regulate or cope with stress flowing from environmental as well as internal sources.
>
> 4. *Feedback.* The capacity of a system to persist in the face of stress is a function of the presence and nature of the information and other influences that return to its actors and decision-makers.[10]

[9] In *The Nerves of Government* (New York: The Free Press of Glencoe, Inc., 1963), Deutsch presents an extremely useful introduction to cybernetics as it relates to the history of what he calls the "Search for Models of Society and Politics." An article representative of the direct effect of cybernetics on thinking about comparative politics is John T. Dorsey, Jr., "An Information-Energy Model," in Ferrel Heady and Sybil L. Stokes, eds., *Papers in Comparative Public Administration* (Ann Arbor, Michigan: Institute of Public Administration, 1962).

[10] David Easton, *A Framework for Political Analysis* (Englewood Cliffs, N.J.: Prentice-Hall, Inc., 1965), p. 25. Compare also Gabriel A. Almond,

Thus is generated a model of the polity as an input-output system, stressed or loaded by interactions with its environment, and responding in a more or less adaptive manner. The system's responses in turn depend in part on the speed and accuracy with which information relevant to past performance can be gathered and assimilated. The cybernetic parentage of such a view of politics is obvious.

Furthermore, even when the systems vocabulary is missing, it is possible to detect the cybernetic ancestry of much recent thinking about the political process. As an example, consider Lasswell's characterization of the decisional sequence:

> Think of any act of decision. We conceive it as beginning in an influx of information from sources at the focus of attention of participants in the decision process, some of whom perceive that their goal values have been or may be affected in ways that can be influenced by community decision. We refer to this as the *intelligence* phase.
>
> The next phase is *recommending,* or promoting, which refers to activities designed to influence the outcome. The *prescribing* phase is the articulation of norms; it includes, for instance, the enacting of enforceable statutes. The *invoking* phase occurs when a prescription is provisionally used to characterize a set of concrete circumstances. When a prescription is employed with finality, we speak of *application.* The *appraisal* phase characterizes the relationship between policy goals and the strategies and results obtained. The *terminating* phase involves the handling of expectations ("rights") established when a prescription was in force.[11]

Again, we can detect in this sequential model the familiar pattern of men interacting with their environment, first to gather information and eventually to evaluate the outcomes of decisions made for the purpose of guiding future decisions.

"A Developmental Approach to Political Systems," *World Politics,* Vol. XVII, No. 2, January 1965, pp. 183-214, and Kuhn, *The Study of Society* (Homewood, Ill.: Dorsey Press, 1963). With respect to fundamentals, the differences between Easton, Almond, and Kuhn are terminological, not conceptual.

[11] Harold D. Lasswell, *The Future of Political Science* (New York: Atherton Press, 1963), pp. 15-16; emphasis in original.

Examples of this sort could be multiplied, but to no particular advantage. At this stage our purpose is not to argue the utility of communication models in comparative politics, but only to suggest that in a very real sense they are already a fact of life in much recent theoretical work. From our point of view this is a distinct advantage because much of the conceptual vocabulary necessary to a communication approach is already partially assimilated into current thinking and dialogue. Concepts such as feedback, channel, network, input, and output now slip easily — perhaps too easily — into discussions about the nature and functioning of the polity. Despite the opportunities for superficiality and even fraud which the new vocabulary affords, the gains far outweigh the dangers and disadvantages, for we have witnessed in the past decade and a half a conceptual movement of sufficient proportions to liberate in the most basic manner our ways of thinking about and viewing the political process.

2. *Field Research in the Sociological Tradition.* Coupled with the rise of macrotheoretical work either in, or of direct relevance to, comparative politics, there has been a shift in the research tradition. For brevity, the newer style of research is here thought of as in the sociological tradition in order to distinguish it from an earlier but still much used approach which might be thought of as in the historical tradition.

The components of the shift in research style are well known. They include movement toward greater reliance on theory in the organization of empirical work, physical movement from the library to the field in the conduct of inquiry, and increased emphasis on the systematic and at times quantitative exploitation of data in the analysis stage.[12] The distinction between the historical and the sociological research traditions is not meant to be invidious. Rather the sociological research tra-

[12] A good, recent example of research in comparative politics which falls squarely into the sociological tradition is Gabriel A. Almond and Sidney Verba, *The Civic Culture: Political Attitudes and Democracy in Five Nations* (Princeton, N.J.: Princeton University Press, 1963). For relevant essays see Robert E. Ward, et. al., *Studying Politics Abroad: Field Research in the Developing Areas* (Boston: Little, Brown and Company, 1964).

dition is closely related in current practice to the conceptual developments noted earlier. Most simply, the new vocabulary necessarily arises from and implies new research procedures and skills. It is very difficult, for example, to investigate response and feedback processes as they affect political decision making, given the procedures and tools usually associated with the historical approach to research.

Of course many of the sociological procedures and skills in use actually predate the conceptual developments to which they are now found applicable. For instance, sample survey methodology was highly developed long before students of comparative politics turned their research attention to questions such as the relationship of system inputs (demands and supports) to system performance, questions on which sample surveys can in fact shed a great deal of light.[13] But for our purposes the *current* availability of both the conceptual vocabulary and the sociological research tradition is what matters. That is, in comparative politics at the present time in addition to a proliferation of models related to communication we have at hand also a nascent research tradition which will enable us to investigate both the viability and the validity of the models. Many of the questions now being asked by the systems theorist are open to investigation in the sociological tradition. This confluence of theory and research bodes well for the future of communication approaches to comparative political study.

3. *Revived Concern with the Proper Organization of Political Life.* Earlier, the rise of Naziism in Germany and Stalinism in the Soviet Union precipitated widespread anxiety over the survival of individual rights in the twentieth century; and more recently, postcolonial developments of an authoritarian cast in parts of Africa and Asia have raised new questions about the viability of democratic institutions in societies oppressed by pervasive shortages of human well-being and political experience. In fact, the diversity and experimentation seen in political systems around the world today, have driven many

[13] See Almond and Verba, *op. cit.,* Frank Bonilla, "Survey Techniques," in Ward, *op. cit.,* and the literature cited therein for examples of the ways in which surveys can be used.

students of comparative politics back to a reconsideration of the basic subjects of the political philosopher: the goals which government should attempt to achieve, the proper relationships of rulers and subjects, and the meaning of concepts such as freedom, justice, and equality.

As is usually recognized, these classical concerns contain an irreducible normative component. That is, the political philosopher as philosopher eventually must attempt to wrestle with questions which involve choices among values. Such choices can be guided by, but not made or justified on, the basis of empirical data alone. When the gap from description of "what is" to prescription for what "ought to be" must be bridged, appeals to the former are not sufficient for constructing linkages to the latter.[14]

To choose just one example, consider the venerable question of how fully the coercive power of the state should be used to force individuals to act "in the public interest." Let us narrow the example and make it more relevant by imagining an African nation in which most of the badly needed foreign exchange is earned by the sale of cocoa. Let us further imagine that existing stands of cocoa are being progressively weakened and killed by a disease for which there is no known control except to cut down and destroy the trees and replace them with a hardier strain.[15] Administrative action directed toward the destruction of the trees is inhibited, however, by the understandable reluctance of the individual farmers to destroy their property (and

[14] Even in analyses of the most rigorous and quantitative kind sooner or later this problem is encountered. See, for example, Hayward R. Alker, Jr., and Bruce M. Russett, "On Measuring Inequality," *Behavioral Science,* Vol. 9, July 1964, pp. 207-218.

[15] Students of African politics will recognize this example as derived from the Ghanaian experience. The disease which plagued the cocoa crop in Ghana is known as "swollen shoot" and in fact can be controlled only by destroying the tree, a practice known locally as "cutting-out." In the fifteen years from 1945 to 1960, more than 95 million cocoa trees in Ghana were destroyed by cutting-out. See Government of Ghana, *Economic Survey, 1960* (Accra: Government Printing Department, 1961), p. 24. The persuasional and educational devices used in the cocoa cutting-out campaigns are described in Peter du Sautoy, *Community Development in Ghana* (London: Oxford University Press, 1958), pp. 150-56, and Appendix V.

their ancestral heritage) for reasons only dimly understood. There can be little quarrel that under accepted economic criteria it is in the interest of almost everyone (including in the long run the farmers themselves) to destroy the diseased trees. But this gives little guidance to those who must enforce the unpopular policy. Education, persuasion, compensation, and bribery (in the form of overpayment or promise of future benefits or privileges) will win the cooperation of a significant fraction of the farmers, but there will remain another group that will yield only to threats, imprisonment, and violence. Finally, there is probably a hard core of farmers willing to die to defend their trees.

The normative aspects of this situation are manifold. If "rational" arguments will not convince the farmers, what forms of trickery, emotionalism, and deceit are justified? What mixture of persuasion and coercion should be applied to the recalcitrant minority? What scope of organization and advocacy should be allowed to opponents of the official government policy? The list could be extended, and each of the questions already posed could be broken down into subsidiary questions, but enough has been said to suggest that even a seemingly routine administrative problem can spawn a host of classical dilemmas.

To return to the more general case, we claim that students of comparative politics are evincing a mounting awareness of the normative components of their subject matter.[16] Problems

16 Nowhere is this more readily seen than in the several volumes of the "Studies in Political Development" sponsored by the Committee on Comparative Politics of the Social Science Research Council. See Lucian W. Pye, ed., *Communications and Political Development* (Princeton, N.J.: Princeton University Press, 1963); Joseph LaPalombara, ed., *Bureaucracy and Political Development* (Princeton, N.J.: Princeton University Press, 1963); and others in the series. Because of the "policy science" orientation of this and much other current work, the increasing awareness of normative problems is to be expected. Writing in the preface to the second volume of the series, LaPalombara sets out this orientation clearly:

. . . there are a number of reasons why the social scientist, particularly the political scientist, must be concerned with the topic which this volume encompasses. We need to know more, for example, about the

involving citizen participation, distribution of political costs and benefits, the role of parties and interest groups in political development, involvement of the military in politics, are all familiar to the contemporary political scientist and all are also problems from which it is difficult to exorcise the normative elements. If, as suggested earlier, the classical subjects of the political philosopher are in part open to restatement as communication problems, and if there is a mounting awareness of normative factors in the study of contemporary political systems, then a communication approach may eventually bridge the old and the new in comparative politics. In fact, as it will be argued in Chapter VIII, viewing normative dilemmas as problems in the organization and control of communication may well be a parsimonious way of comparing and contrasting total systems.

Comparative politics, then, as currently studied incorporates models, research strategies, and problem areas on which the latent imprint of a communication approach is already stamped. Subsequent chapters will amplify and make more concrete many of these points. But first we must consider the question that was raised earlier: In the face of empirical, conceptual, and bibliographical superabundance, by what criteria do we limit the scope of our inquiry? It is to this problem that we now turn.

---

various ways in which public bureaucracies can be more or less effective as instruments of change. Additionally — and this is frankly a central concern of those involved in this venture — we wish to have more reliable knowledge about the consequences of certain patterns of change for the probable evolution of democratic polities. Thus, we are asking not merely where the developing new states may be going politically but how development might be pushed in the direction of freedom rather than tyranny. — *Ibid.*, pp. ix-x.

The example of the cocoa trees given in the text illustrates how "freedom rather than tyranny" might be translated into a set of empirical-normative questions.

CHAPTER II

What Communication
Is Most Relevant?

THE ELEMENTS OF A COMMUNICATION MODEL

ALMOST ALL political behavior involves communication activity of some sort. Yet in comparative politics we cannot study all of this activity. Somehow we must narrow the scope of our inquiry; we must establish some priorities. In order to begin the search for boundaries, let us examine the elements of a simple communication model.

As a beginning, we can formalize the Lasswellian paradigm introduced in Chapter I: Who Says What, In Which Channel, To Whom, With What Effect? Translating this from a set of questions into the elements of a more general model, we can say that every act of human communication involves a *source* generating a *message* which travels through a *channel* to an *audience*.[1] (For the moment we shall not consider the question

[1] Compare Wilbur Schramm, "How Communication Works," in Wilbur Schramm, ed., *The Process and Effects of Mass Communication* (Urbana, Ill.: University of Illinois Press, 1955). In this usage a message is a signal or set of signals, ink on paper, sound waves in the air, impulses in an electric current, a wave of the hand. What this message *means*, however, is quite another question. Meanings depend on the interpretations given to the signals by the audience. For a thought-provoking discussion of the range of meanings which can be attached to political events and the consequences for the political system of this interpretive diversity, see Murray Edelman,

17

of effects, which takes us away from an examination of the *process* of communication and into an examination of its *consequences*). Notice that with these four elements we can describe a vast variety of communicatory situations. When a boy whispers "I love you" to his girl friend, all the elements are present. Similarly, when Fidel Castro addresses the Cuban masses on television we can also identify all four elements of the model. In both cases the structure of the communication process is the same although the sources, messages, channels, and audiences involved are quite different.

It takes no special insight to recognize that Castro addressing the masses is an instance of "political communication" whereas the boy whispering to his girl is not.[2] What differentiates the former episode from the latter? Most clearly, it is that Castro is the top political figure in Cuba and that he is talking about politics to the citizenry. In this case, source, message, channel, and audience are all in some direct sense political. But when the boy whispers to the girl, none of these conditions applies.

However, the easy distinction drawn between these two examples, a distinction based on the political-nonpolitical nature of the elements of the model, gives small cause for comfort, because if we try to apply this approach generically to the identification of episodes of political communication we run into problems.

Consider the elements of the model one by one. Does the role or position occupied by the *source* determine whether or not communicatory activity is political? That is, when the President of the United States speaks — no matter what the channel, the message or the audience — is this political communication? Or, to continue, does the content of the *message*

The Symbolic Uses of Politics (Urbana, Ill.: University of Illinois Press, 1964). Readers unfamiliar with the vocabulary of the study of communication will find helpful the essays in Wilbur Schramm, ed., *The Science of Human Communication* (New York: Basic Books, Inc., 1963).

[2] The phrase "political communication" is used here as a shorthand way of referring to that subset of communicatory activity which is especially relevant to an understanding of political life. An informal *definition* of political communication will be offered in the next section of this chapter.

itself — no matter what the source, the channel, or the audience — determine which communications are political? When two teenagers talk about a forthcoming election, is this political communication? Or is it the *channel* that counts? Just because the state owns the television networks in the Soviet Union is every minute of Russian television to be considered political communication? And finally, what about the *audience?* Should all communication activity directed to political role holders be considered political communication?

The obvious answer to every one of the above questions is "no." That is, we cannot, or at least we should not, identify instances of political communication simply according to the sources, messages, channels, or audiences involved. We should not be bound to an approach which instructs us to take notice every time the President compliments his wife, a teenager mentions the election to a friend, Soviet television presents a light drama, or an office boy says good morning to a senator.

A FUNCTIONAL APPROACH TO COMMUNICATION

What has happened, of course, is that we are facing in the field of communication a variation of one of the most enduring problems of the study of politics, the definition of the components and boundaries of the political system itself. As is well known, it is frequently difficult and at times impossible to say in the abstract whether or not individual A or institution X is part of the political system. It all depends on what A and X are doing. If A is a truck driver he is "in" the system when he is voting and "out" when he is playing catch with his son. If X is A's union, it is "in" when lobbying for new highway construction and "out" when organizing the annual picnic.

Similarly, common sense tells us that the President complimenting his wife is probably not communicatory activity which should be considered "in" the system, but when he holds a news conference it is. Or to choose an institutional focus, *The New York Times'* page devoted to betrothals and marriages does not seem like political communication, but, on the other hand, a *Times'* editorial critique of American foreign policy does. What is the basis for the distinction suggested here? Most simply, that *communicatory activity is considered political by virtue of the consequences, actual and potential, that it has for the functioning of the political system.*[3]

This emphasis on consequences and political functioning does not mean that we can now forget about sources, messages, channels, and audiences. Quite the contrary, these elements are of prime importance in determining the probability that the communication in question will have consequences for political functioning. A remark made by Walter Lippmann in his nationally syndicated newspaper column is clearly of a political potential quite different from the same remark made by a college professor to a friend over cocktails. But no matter what the source, message, channel, or audience, it is to the political consequences of the communicatory activity that we must look as the final basis for judgment in those instances when the structure and content of communication may mislead us.

A few examples may help to clarify the point. Suppose that the President and his wife have a serious marital spat in public. This otherwise private matter becomes political by virtue of the channels activated and the norms and operating rules of the American political system. Because of the characteristics of public communication in the United States, we can expect an outpouring of interpretive and augmentative messages about the event. Because of the importance of appearances in the Presidential office, we can imagine that the event will cause a palpable dropping away of support (perhaps disastrous at election time) for the President and his policies, even though there is no demonstrated relationship between marital happiness and public competence. Or consider a situation in which neither source, message, channel, or audience is overtly political. Hyman argues that the "package" of manifestly nonpolitical mass communication presented to audiences in the less developed countries nevertheless has important consequences for political change. That is, by watching even such vulgar fare as the English-language horror, love, and adventure films widely circulated in Asia and Africa, the new citizens of these nations

---

[3] Indirectly, we have now incorporated *effects,* the fifth element of the Lasswellian paradigm into our discussion.

come to develop skills and attitudes of political relevance.[4] Notice that this insight is by no means completely fresh. The possible consequences of manifestly nonpolitical artistic communication are well understood by absolutist rulers who strive to control cultural life lest the tastes and habits of independence and self-expression formed there carry over into political life.

This approach to the study of political communication suggests an investigatory sequence. First we want to bound and examine the operation of the political system. (Here is where the primary burden of concept formation and definition falls.) Then we isolate the communication processes crucial to an understanding of the system's functioning. Finally we search for the sources, messages, meanings, channels, audiences, and their relationships which, taken together, are necessary for an understanding of the communication processes. This approach has the great virtue of turning problems of definition into empirical problems.[5] That is, when one asks functional questions, one is in a sense seeking the operative elements of the system with full realization that these elements and their relationships differ among systems and also change with the passing of time in the same system. As an example, if we ask how the young become socialized to politics — how they acquire the skills and attitudes necessary for political participation — we find an empirical range which includes such diverse institutions as the Boy Scouts, the British public school, and the

[4] See Herbert Hyman, "Mass Media and Political Socialization: The Role of Patterns of Communication," in Lucian W. Pye, ed., *Communications and Political Development* (Princeton, N.J.: Princeton University Press, 1963).

[5] On the boundaries of the political system see David Easton, *A Framework for Political Analysis* (Englewood Cliffs, N.J.: Prentice-Hall, Inc., 1965), particularly chapter Four, "The Identification of the Political System." On the functional approach (or approaches) to the study of politics, see Gabriel A. Almond and G. Bingham Powell, *Comparative Politics: A Developmental Approach* (Boston: Little, Brown and Company, forthcoming), particularly Chapter II and the literature cited therein. Useful for this discussion and not cited by Almond and Powell is Charles R. Wright. "Functional Analysis and Mass Communication," *Public Opinion Quarterly*, Vol. XXIV, No. 4, Winter 1960, pp. 605-620.

Cuban people's militia. If we then focus in detail on the Scouts, the school, and the militia, we can ask a host of narrower process questions suggested by our model of the elements of all communicatory activity. Thus, we do not ask in the first instance whether the institutions are formally within or outside of the political system, but rather in what way they are important to its operation.

It is important to realize that although we focus on the system effects of communicatory activity, we are not bound to any particular taxonomy of political functions. In a special version of the "everything in politics is communication" argument, Almond has noted,

> All of the functions performed in the political system — political socialization and recruitment, interest articulation, interest aggregation, rule-making, rule application, and rule adjudication — are performed *by means* of communication. Parents, teachers, and priests, for example, impart political socialization through communication. Interest group leaders and representatives and party leaders perform their articulation and aggregation functions by communicating demands and policy recommendations. Legislators enact laws on the basis of information communicated to them and by communicating with one another and with other elements of the political system. In performing their functions, bureaucrats receive and analyze information from the society and from various parts of the polity. Similarly, the judicial process is carried on by means of communication.[6]

Clearly there is nothing final or sacred about this functional array. (In his current work Almond has changed and elaborated it.) Moreover, the ubiquity of communication as a process remains even if this taxonomy is refined or replaced. We can thus agree on the importance of treating as central the system consequences of communication without being in full prior

[6] Gabriel A. Almond, "Introduction," in Gabriel A. Almond and James S. Coleman, eds., *The Politics of the Developing Areas* (Princeton, N.J.: Princeton University Press, 1960), pp. 4-5; emphasis in original. Almond, in developing his argument, comes to consider political communication a function separate from and coequal with the other six, a view not shared here.

agreement on the components of a functional theory of the polity.

THE FOCUS ON COMPARATIVE MACROANALYSIS

However, as the above passage suggests, in favoring a definition of political communication that emphasizes system consequences rather than sources, messages, channels, and audiences, we have clearly not yet fully escaped from the "everything in politics is communication" trap. If we remain at the most abstract level of thinking about politics and communication, there is no way further to limit the potential subjects to which we might be led. For the purposes of theory construction this may be a strength rather than a weakness. But, unfortunately, paths through the substantive and bibliographical jungle described in Chapter I cannot be charted by appeals to conceptual signposts alone; dirtier work is called for. Thus it is time to start swinging the machete, and much of the remainder of this book represents the results of such an effort.

But before beginning, it is wise to recall just what we are trying to do. Remember that we are here interested in the study of communication only to the extent that it aids us in the *comparative* study of *national* political systems. Thus, we set high priority on the study of macropatterns and activities of communication and their gross consequences for the functioning of the national system.[7] We are attempting to so characterize these communication patterns, activities, and consequences as to facilitate national comparison; and, because of the empirical diversity with which we must ultimately deal, the initial analytical net must not catch and hold all communication activity, even though that activity may have functional relevance. Much must be allowed to slip through, thus sharply curtailing the empirical materials of immediate interest. Two examples may help to clarify the point: A study of the communication patterns operating in legislature X during the pas-

----

[7] This statement masks a problem of substantial complexity and importance. See Heinz Eulau, *The Behavioral Persuasion in Politics* (New York: Random House, Inc., 1963), "Macro-Micro Dilemmas," pp. 123-27 and passim.

sage of bill Y may well be legitimate and useful research in many contexts; but unless it can be shown that the patterns revealed are somehow characteristic of legislature X when engaged in rule making and unless it further can be shown that these patterns are of large enough scale to facilitate comparison across different systems, the research is of little value for our purposes. Or in another vein, much of what passes as research into public opinion, if uninformed by theoretical considerations and not thrown into relief by parallel work in other polities, contributes almost nothing to comparative political study as here understood.

Comparative macroanalysis based on a mapping of enduring large-scale communication patterns is by no means as unusual or esoteric as the terminology might lead one to believe. We are all familiar with discussions of democracy, autocracy, and totalitarianism; such discussions pervade the literature of politics. Without attempting to defend this scheme of classification, let us characterize in the simplest possible language each type of system as a certain way of organizing communications and political life, as a certain way of answering six questions.[8] For reasons which will become obvious, the democratic type will be reclassified into two subtypes, classical democracy and compromise democracy.

CLASSICAL DEMOCRACY

1. *How Are the Leaders Chosen and Changed?* All full citizens choose from among their number amateurs to oversee the conduct of political affairs. The overseers are chosen in a one-man, one-vote election. Periodically, a new group of amateurs is elected, and members of the retiring group return to their original status as citizens. Competition for the role of overseer or supervisor is minimal because the advantages of office are few and all who are qualified and wish to assume the responsibility will eventually have the opportunity to serve.

[8] Echoes and elaborations of some of the six points will be found in Chapter VIII. The four types presented are incomplete and very gross idealizations or abstractions, constructed for illustrative purposes. They should not be understood as descriptions of real systems. Both abstract normative and abstract descriptive elements are included.

2. *Who Defines Political Problems and Alternatives?* The citizens, meeting in public, debate the problems facing the political system and hear grievances and proposals for action and reform. Every citizen has the right to propose, advocate, and defend his chosen position or the position of the group in whose name he speaks. The overseers confine their participation to the maintenance of proper procedure, except in issue areas in which the citizens may not possess sufficient information to initiate debate.

3. *Who Participates in Making Public Policy?* Once alternative responses to policy questions have been posed, the citizens choose by voting from among the alternatives before them. Again, the one-man, one-vote rule operates, and it is assumed that, when more than two alternatives have been posed, a plurality will be sufficient to decide the question.

4. *What Is the Scope of Allowable Criticism?* During the definition of political problems and the posing of alternatives, any criticism which does not violate "the canons of good taste and of the community" is allowable. Once public policy has been decided upon, however, it is not legitimate to obstruct by word or deed its implementation. Criticism of existing policy must be brought into the public forum to generate a revised plan of action or reform. Once in the public forum, the criticism will trigger the processes described under (2) and (3) above; if sufficient support can be won, the criticism will take effect in the form of new public policy.

5. *How Do Citizens Become Informed about the Politically Relevant World?* The citizen informs himself by attendance at the forum, by participation in public life, by civilized and inquiring conversation with his peers, and by reading and study when appropriate materials are available. It is a prime purpose of education to equip the citizen to so inform himself and thus be prepared to make humane and measured civic judgments. With respect to materials which are germane to public issues but not readily available, it is the duty of the overseers to provide the relevant information to the citizenry.

6. *Who May Choose to Isolate Himself from Politics?* The good citizen participates to the limits of his time, energy, and

knowledge in the political process. Although withdrawal from
political life does not subject one to formal sanctions or punishment, it is inconceivable that the really virtuous or enlightened
man would want to withdraw; for, in a system so organized,
both civic duty and self-interest dictate the continued participation of the citizen in decisions which are linked directly to
his needs and preferences.

Summary. In the classical democracy, most communication
flows in a circular manner in and among the citizenry while
debate, discussion, public criticism, and finally group decision
take place. Because there is minimal differentiation in decisional power between the citizens and their elected supervisors,
communication down the hierarchy is of an informational
rather than a directive type. It is designed to place at the disposal of the citizens the facts needed to ensure thorough discussion and wise decision. Thus the citizen is at liberty to ignore
this communication, although civic training and self-interest
suggest that he will not. Communication up the hierarchy,
from citizen to overseer, takes the form of policy decisions,
which it is the task of the overseer to implement.

COMPROMISE DEMOCRACY

1. *How Are the Leaders Chosen and Changed?* Competition
for high public office in free, open, and periodic elections is a
prominent feature of the political landscape. Lesser offices are
filled by appointment on the basis of technical qualifications
or previous services rendered. The advantages of public office
are great, occasioning an electoral struggle more massive than
anything imagined in classical democracy. The contest for public office gives rise to political organizations which specialize
in the creation and maintenance of popular support.

2. *Who Defines Political Problems and Alternatives?* The
political elite enjoy certain very decided advantages in the
defining of political problems and the scheduling of alternatives. However, the citizens, at times acting directly but usually
acting through the individuals or groups representing them,
also have important prerogatives. Ideally, any citizen with a
problem or an alternative has the right to be heard, but in

practice it is recognized that only groups can command the resources and attention necessary to make their weight felt in the political arena.[9] It follows that the so-called "independent" media of communication contribute heavily to both the defining and the scheduling of problems and alternatives.

3. *Who Participates in the Making of Public Policy?* The comments under (2) apply, with the added condition that the second, third, and lesser levels of officialdom are critically important in the making of policy because only they have access to the information and expertise necessary to draw up operational plans. At the final stage, the representatives and perhaps the executive move to the forefront because formal power of decision is vested in them.

4. *What Is the Scope of Allowable Criticism?* The scope is very great, almost without limits. The law of sedition is evoked to punish, if at all, only in periods of high emergency, and treason is defined by actions rather than words. However, in practice the right to criticize is necessarily bounded when other rights such as public order, reputation, property, and privacy are infringed. Because of the scale of politics, the individual citizen cannot usually be overly effective in criticizing govern-

---

[9] Robert A. Dahl has captured the core of this argument well:

I defined the "normal" American political process as one in which there is a high probability that an active and legitimate group in the population can make itself heard effectively at some crucial stage in the process of decision. To be "heard" covers a wide range of activities, and I do not intend to define the word rigorously. Clearly, it does not mean that every group has equal control over the outcome.

. . . When I say that a group is heard "effectively" I mean more than the simple fact that it makes a noise; I mean that one or more officials are not only ready to listen to the noise, but expect to suffer in some significant way if they do not placate the group, its leaders, or its most vociferous members. — *A Preface to Democratic Theory* (Chicago: University of Chicago Press, 1956), p. 145.

I have used Dahl's model of polyarchal democracy as an aid in developing what is here called compromise democracy. Also, his model of populistic democracy has been useful in thinking about classical democracy, although the small-scale Greek idealization is actually closer to what I have in mind in the latter case.

ment. Thus, the press (mass media) is thought of as a "fourth branch" of government which makes sure that the other three perform as they should; the media are the eyes and the ears of the people, the watchdog set out to guard the republic. In order to provide such service, it is necessary that the media be as well insulated from government as possible.

5. *How Do Citizens Become Informed about the Politically Relevant World?* The world is so complex and distant and the citizen so busy and otherwise preoccupied that the major burden of making available relevant political information falls to the mass media. But the government too has a continuing responsibility in this area, for it must make known to the people the laws, directives, and policies with which it expects them to comply. It is impossible (and probably not desirable) for every citizen to become well informed on every issue and subject; the uneven distribution of time, interest, and resources among the citizenry leads to an uneven distribution of information. Nevertheless, when a citizen or group is motivated to participate in debate or decision making on public policy, the general availability of information should be such that relevant facts are easy to find.

6. *Who May Choose to Isolate Himself from Politics?* Any citizen may withdraw from political life as long as he continues to comply with the laws and directives promulgated by the duly constituted powers.

Summary. The most dominant characteristic of compromise democracy is its complexity. This, of course, is reflected in its major communication patterns which are of at least five types. First is a continuing flow within and between the various branches and agencies of government as the business of politics is carried on. Second is the flow from government to citizens designed to elicit support and to promulgate and implement public policy. Third is the flow among the citizens as political groupings are formed and as those with common problems and interests seek each other out in preparation for political activity. Fourth is the shifting and multichanneled flow from the citizens (or nongovernmental groups) to representatives and officials. Here, demands, preferences, and criticism are communicated up the hierarchy reflecting changes in the scope and subject matter of popular participation. Fifth is the three-way flow between government, the citizenry, and the mass media, with the media acting as watchdog and neutral source of information both for government and for the people. In the abstract, it is difficult to say which of these patterns is quantitatively or qualitatively most important to the operation of the system.

AUTOCRACY

1. *How Are the Leaders Chosen and Changed?* Ideally, the leadership perpetuates itself, either by inheritance or by the elevation of the next in line. However, in practice interelite struggle for high office is frequently a chief characteristic of the system. Coup, assassination, and forced retirement are three of the ways in which the struggle may be manifested; but, struggle or not, the masses are not brought into the process of choice in any standardized way except as their kinetic energy may prove useful to one or another faction. And, of course, there is no regular and periodic change of leadership; turnovers occur when precipitated by death, schism, or other unscheduled events.

2. *Who Defines Political Problems and Alternatives?* The effective insulation of the elite from demands which originate among the masses is a defining characteristic of autocracy. In one form or another, "Let them eat cake" is the timeless autocratic response to popular cries for bread. Attempts by citizens or groups to bring problems to the attention of decision makers are met with one of several strategies, all designed to preserve elite prerogatives: A hearing is granted but no action is taken, the protesting or petitioning group is ignored or discredited, a "circus" is offered to divert public attention, or force and repression are used.

3. *Who Participates in the Making of Public Policy?* It is here that the elitism of the autocracy shows itself most clearly. Even should the citizens manage to bring their demands to the attention of the elite, the latter will not allow the former to participate in the making of policy which bears on the issues at stake. That those with political power can no longer ignore a problem is no guarantee that they will bring those most af-

fected by the problem into consultation, unless of course those most affected on closer inspection turn out to be relatives, cronies, or a potential counterelite.

4. *What Is the Scope of Allowable Criticism?* Needless to say, the scope of allowable criticism is extremely narrow, in many areas nonexistent. The standard method of limiting public criticism is punitive: citizens, groups, and media that step out of line are subjected to swift and severe punishment. The punishment is meant to be deterrent as well as retributive. Thus, although licensing, censorship, and harassment are used to contain those who would speak out against the regime or its policies, the most important mechanism of control is fear of incurring the displeasure of the rulers with all that might follow in physical and fiscal discomfort.

5. *How Do Citizens Become Informed about the Politically Relevant World?* Because so much of politics is "not their business," the citizens have minimal need for information other than what is necessary for compliance. The government assumes responsibility for promulgating the laws and dicta which it expects the people to obey. The mass media are either captive and thus cooperate in the promulgation of government information, or they are effectively neutralized by fear of reprisal and thus steer clear of all potentially sensitive subjects.

6. *Who May Choose to Isolate Himself from Politics?* The good citizen minds his own business and does as he is told. Except on certain ceremonial occasions when he is expected to appear in the plaza to cheer or in the voting booth to validate the prescribed ticket, he is allowed and in fact encouraged or required to withdraw from political activity. As long as he causes no trouble for the regime (and trouble is very broadly defined), the rulers and their agents will usually leave him alone.

Summary. Among the elite and governing circles of an autocracy there are complex and continuing flows of communication as factions jostle for power, issues are raised, and decisions are made. Similarly, the flow of communication down the hierarchy to the masses is continuous, at least in systems where the content of public policy is both rich and variable enough to make mass compliance a problem. But noticeably lacking is communication up the hierarchy in the form of criticism and participation in decision making or the choice of leaders. Because the people have no voice in government and cannot band together for political purposes, little intercitizen communication takes place. Except for the pervasive popular grumbling which is either too costly or impossible to suppress, there is a pervading political stillness about the land. Thus, except at the highest reaches of society, autocracy is a "quiet" system, the quietest of the four types here considered.

TOTALITARIANISM

1. *How Are the Leaders Chosen and Changed?* As in autocracy, the leadership perpetuates itself without reference either to the wishes of the citizenry or to a prearranged schedule of replacement in office. The ruling party maintains a complete monopoly over positions of political importance, and aspirants for high office must climb the party hierarchy on their way to power; there is no other ladder. Thus, tomorrow's leaders are predictably men with substantial political experience, tempered in the struggle for power, and possessing a firm grasp of how the system works. This recruitment pattern lends a degree of continuity and stability to totalitarian politics that is lacking in nonmonarchic autocracy.

2. *Who Defines Political Problems and Alternatives?* The party leadership reserves to itself the right to say what is and is not an issue. As makers, keepers, and interpreters of the official doctrine, the leadership is able not only to refuse the masses the opportunity to press demands on the government, but also to deny the legitimacy and even the reality of the demands themselves. When unwanted issues obtrude despite attempts of the elite to suppress or deny them, the doctrine is reinterpreted or expanded to take cognizance of the new problems. Thus the leadership is able to coopt persistent demands, integrate them into the doctrine, and as a consequence defuse the masses by stealing their fire.

3. *Who Participates in the Making of Public Policy?* In common with all complex systems, bureaucratic officials in totalitarianism are important in the policy-making process because only they command the expertise needed to give opera-

tional form to abstract ideas. But the party elites maintain tight control over subsidiary processes of decision, and it is they who set out the political guidelines within which the technocrats must operate. Finally, the finished product may be given to the citizenry or to a "people's assembly" to endorse by acclamation, but it cannot be said that the citizens have thereby shaped in any meaningful way the policies which they have been called upon to ratify.

4. *What Is the Scope of Allowable Criticism?* At no time are the content of public policy and the men who are responsible for its creation open to popular criticism. In the implementation stage, however, both the manner of administration and the practice of the administrators are fair game for the critics, as long as the criticism does not even by inference impugn the virtue or wisdom of those who hold political power. In this way the holiness of the master plan and the master planners is preserved, for whatever discontent is generated by the enforcement of current dogma is attributed to the incompetence of the lesser functionaries rather than to the unsoundness or malevolence of the program itself. The mass media, of course, are closely linked adjuncts of the ruling party, and no trace of critical comment (except as ordered from above) is to be found therein.

5. *How Do Citizens Become Informed about the Politically Relevant World?* Unlike autocracy, wherein politics is not the business of the ordinary citizen, in totalitarianism an attempt is made to extend the scope of governmental activity until almost all social routines are drawn into the political sphere. Thus every citizen must have a full understanding of what is to be done and the part which he will play in the new order. Organic to this massive effort at social change and control is a massive program of political communication. Every conceivable long channel in the society is at the service of the elite in this effort. The mass media, the schools, the armed forces, the party, and mass organizations such as the labor unions are all used to blanket the countryside with approved information and exhortation.

6. *Who May Choose to Isolate Himself from Politics?* As im-

plied in the previous section, the good citizen in the totalitarian system does much more than simply obey the laws and stay out of trouble. Popular passivity is anathema to the regime, and withdrawal from participation is taken as *prima facie* evidence of disloyalty. As in classical democracy, to give oneself to the polity is considered the highest form of virtue. However, in the totalitarian case the frenzy of participation in approved activities does not issue in increased ability to influence political outcomes. Quite the contrary: the more fully the citizen participates in the prescribed manner, the more he contributes to the perpetuation of a system which effectively denies him a voice in politics.

Summary. The most salient characteristic of totalitarianism is the massive amount of communication which flows from the party elite and their agents to the masses. All the human and technological apparatus controlled by the leadership is designed to achieve maximum public coverage and effectiveness. The effort is continuous, homogeneous, and pervasive. Of course there are other important flows: up the hierarchy in the form of information and low-level criticism and horizontally in leadership and decisional circles in the manner characteristic of all complex bureaucratic systems. But the dominant flow is downward. The self-appointed guardians of the faith bend every effort to ensure that the masses are completely absorbed into the goals of the state as they, the guardians, define those goals. This relationship between leaders and the led implies a network of public communication quite unlike that found in any other system.

As will be argued throughout, and particularly in the final chapter, typologies such as this prove to be of limited usefulness when fine distinctions between real systems must be drawn. They do serve, however, to suggest how intimately patterns of communication are linked to the conduct and understanding of national politics. With this background in mind, we can now proceed to examine in more detail some of the topics and problems with which a communication approach to comparative politics must wrestle.

CHAPTER III

The Components
of Communication Networks

LET US imagine, for a moment, that we could inject into a political system something like the fluorescent tracers used by doctors in medical diagnosis. Our imaginary fluorescent would be designed to follow the primary channels of political communication. If we were then to put a political system under the fluoroscope and throw the switch, what would we see?

In the first place, the view would depend on which system was on the table. If it were Cuba, we would discover that a host of mass organizations, the military, the mass media, the party, the schools, and special structures such as the "Committees for the Defense of the Revolution" are used extensively for vertical communication in the system.[1] We would find also a great deal of lateral communication and structural overlap among a rather compact group of party members and top bureaucrats. On the other hand, if the system being examined were the United States, we would get a different picture. Here

[1] Committees for the Defense of the Revolution were first formed by Castro in 1960 to act as a grass-roots defense against counterrevolutionaries. Organized on a geographical basis, they soon became multipurpose citizen groups used by the leadership for recruiting, administering, and proselytizing in the service of the revolution.

we would find prominently featured as vertical channels the bureaucracy, various types of interest groups, the mass media, and, intermittently, the political parties. Lateral flows would occur at a great many levels, and the networks within and between important institutions such as the Congress and the State Department would be highly complex.

To continue the image for a moment, the fluoroscopic picture of either system would be altered drastically if we were to catch it in a period of crisis or high excitement. This is a matter which will be examined in detail in Chapter V, but it is well to touch on it here. Even in the least complex political systems there are channels which are not normally used but which can be activated under the impact of certain events. In highly complex systems, the differences are well illustrated by imagining the peculiarities revealed if the United States were put under the fluoroscope during a presidential campaign. Certainly anyone mapping communication in and around the party structures and personalities during the campaign would err greatly if he assumed that the observed patterns were characteristic of the modal daily operation of the system. Similarly, in Cuba immediately before and after the Bay of Pigs invasion, channels were activated that had been dormant or quiescent during times when revolutionary politics was functioning as usual.

The more general point is that there is some structural elasticity in the communication patterns observed in any political system at different points of time. The picture revealed by our fluoroscope depends greatly on when we catch the system — with what political problems it is occupied at the time. Always we will observe some core channels in operation, the channels which may be thought of as carrying on the system's continuing political business. In addition we will observe specialized channels, activated in response to special problems and events.

Lest this notion of structural elasticity cause confusion, it should be pointed out that we are not now talking about growth or development of the total communication capacity of political systems. This topic will be treated in Chapter VII;

but, in the interest of clarification, a preliminary word is in order here. Some theorists see political development principally in a system's increased capacity to extend national communication networks (and all that this implies) into new sectors of the society. These theorists also view the penetration of previously isolated local and traditional communication structures by the national system as requisites of political development. These are important ideas and deserve careful consideration, but at the moment we are concerned only with suggesting that, in response to changing circumstances, all political systems, whether undergoing rapid transformation or not, exhibit changes in the channels and networks that are in use.

Passing on from the metaphor of the fluoroscope and the patternings of political communication that it might reveal, let us examine types of channels in actual systems. Here we are concerned with what structures and institutions in the society are, or might be, used to carry on communication of consequence to the gross functioning of the political system. A fourfold classification is used: (1) organizations, (2) groups, (3) the mass media, and (4) special channels for interest articulation and aggregation. The classification is not intended to be either exhaustive or conceptually elegant. Rather, its aim is to order in a preliminary manner the diversity of channels and to suggest possible structural points of similarity and difference among systems.

One other word of warning: The typology draws no hard and fast distinction between structures having communication as their primary function and those for which communication is ancillary to other activities. It is tempting at times to isolate the mass media and think of them as somehow the purest and most specialized communication structures; but such a view overlooks the fact that organizations such as the Leninist party are in their own way just as specialized and just as singlemindedly concerned with communication as are the mass media. One way of summarizing the position taken here is to note that the primary function of the mass media is *always* communication, whereas such may not be the case in relevant organizations, groups, and special channels.

ORGANIZATIONS AS CHANNELS

As we have already suggested, among the most important political communication channels are institutions such as parties, interest groups, public bureaucracies, unions, and mass organizations capable of linking the elite, the subelite, and broad sectors of the citizenry. We refer to institutions of this sort, national or nearly national in scope and significance, permanent or semipermanent in structure, although not necessarily continuous in operation, as organizational channels.

The comparative study of these channels should take into account at least the following three points.

1. *Organizational Channels of Political Consequence Are Not Necessarily Part of the Political System in the Structural Sense.* This is a restatement of a position taken earlier, but it is well to re-emphasize it here. The basic point is that important organizational channels may not be part of what is normally thought of as the political system. For example, schools and unions in the United States are outside the political system in the structural sense, but at times they function as important channels of political communication. In other systems, the political use of nonpolitical channels is more continuous and complete. Thus Millen, writing about ostensibly independent labor unions in the developing countries, notes:

> The function most expected of the union is that of providing a channel of communication between the political elite — which may be the government in power or a party in opposition — and the masses. In the best situations the channel is two-way. . . . To be effective in this channeling function, a union must have the widest possible mass character, and it must have means for mobilizing its indoctrinated membership or sympathizers for action on command.[2]

The situation referred to by Millen differs from that in the fully developed Leninist system in which governmental penetration and control of unions and other institutions are so

[2] Bruce H. Millen, *The Political Role of Labor in Developing Countries* (Washington, D.C.: The Brookings Institution, 1963), p. 83.

complete that those organizations *are* structurally within the political system. In our view, the Leninist system defines one end of a continuum, the end at which few if any organizational channels of political consequence are autonomous. Under the totalitarian "passion for unanimity," all possible organizational channels are incorporated into the political system.[3] But there are other, increasingly noninclusive, structural formats arrayed along the continuum. One task of comparative analysis is to sort out and describe these other formats.

2. *The Political Use of Organizational Channels Is Intermittent or Partial in Many Instances.* Again, this has been touched on previously but bears repeating here. The intermittency may be of two forms. The first is exemplified by the labor union which sometimes serves as a political channel and at other times (or at the same time) performs economic functions such as the training of new workers. This is an example of the multifunctionality of most complex organizations. The second form of intermittency is shown by structures that almost entirely cease to operate when not functioning primarily as channels of political communication. Political parties in some Latin American countries illustrate the type. The key point is that, although the skeleton of the party continues to exist between elections, it is only when the contest is joined that communication, or any activity of major political consequence, takes place. Political parties in the United States operate somewhat in this manner, although their degree of interelection quiescence does not approach the Latin American type.

3. *Organizational Channels Differ Widely in the Political Communication Uses Which They Serve.* This is a version of one of the most widely accepted canons of modern political analysis. The parent proposition reminds us that nominal and structural similarities are a poor guide to political functioning, that the Italian Communist Party and the Chinese Communist Party, despite structural similarities, fit into the operation of

[3] Among others, see Carl J. Friedrich and Zbigniew K. Brzezinski, *Totalitarian Dictatorship and Autocracy* (New York: Frederick A. Praeger, Inc., 1961), particularly Part IV.

the Italian and Chinese political systems in quite different ways. Likewise, we should not assume that observed structural similarities in organizational channels give us a firm basis for inferring similarities in political functions performed. The basic structures of the Soviet and American public school systems are not dissimilar, but the former is more overtly conceived of and used as a channel for political communication than the latter. In fact, the continuing battle in the United States between those who would teach more "Americanism" in the classroom and those who would mute the issue is, in part, a controversy over the extent to which this organizational channel should be brought explicitly into the service of the political system. The important point is that organizational channels in most systems have substantial flexibility and unused potentiality for political communication. The uses to which channels are put depend not so much on their structural characteristics as on the purposes to which political leaders wish to see them put within the constraints imposed by political, social, and economic environments. This point will be explored more fully in the next chapter.

GROUPS AS CHANNELS

The line between an organization and a group, as the words are used here, is not easy to draw. By groups we mean those less permanent, less institutionalized, and frequently less pervasive collectivities which sometimes figure prominently in patterns of political communication. At our terminological extremes, the American Medical Association is clearly an organization and the local "housewives for Johnson" is clearly a group, but discrimination would be more difficult in other examples.

Central to the distinction is the notion that communication in a group is less formal than in an organization, and thus group membership must remain compact enough to allow this looser patterning of communication to endure. Organizations, of course, always contain a number of groups within them, and it is on this basis that the frequently drawn dichotomy between "formal" and "informal" channels of organizational communication rests. The organization is defined by its formal channels of communication, so some theorists say, and it survives and functions because of the informal channels which spring up both to sustain social groupings and to bypass and supplement hierarchical arrangements. This distinction is not the only one which is central to our argument. We are concerned also with those informal patternings of communication which are *not* embedded in organizations and thus would not show up if we confined our analysis to the group structure of organizational life.

The most familiar example of the primacy of groups in political communication comes from the literature on American voting behavior. Study after study has demonstrated that at election time communication flows not only from the mass media directly to the individual voter, but also from person to person in the face-to-face groups of family and friends to which the citizen belongs.[4] Moreover, it has been argued, the communication of highest political relevance — in the sense that it is the communication which most affects the voting choice — is that which takes place within these groups. It is there that attitudes are formed and changed and choices are made and reinforced.

Nor need we confine our examples to voting for, as other authors have pointed out, groups perform critical communication functions in almost any process of decision that we might wish to examine.[5] From the highest to the lowest levels of the

[4] See particularly Paul F. Lazarsfeld, Bernard Berelson, and Hazel Gaudet, *The People's Choice* (New York: Columbia University Press, 1948), and Bernard R. Berelson, Paul F. Lazarsfeld, and William N. McPhee, *Voting: A Study of Opinion Formation in a Presidential Campaign* (Chicago: University of Chicago Press, 1954). Additional bibliography and insights can be found in Elihu Katz, "The Two-Step Flow of Communication: An Up-To-Date Report on an Hypothesis," *Public Opinion Quarterly*, Vol. XXI, No. 1, Spring 1957, pp. 61-78.

[5] For an excellent overview of the literature on the importance of groups in the political process see Sidney Verba, *Small Groups and Political Behavior* (Princeton, N.J.: Princeton University Press, 1961), particularly Chapter II, "The Primary Group and Politics." Verba's definition differs from ours in that he includes as groups those small decisional units operating with face-to-face communication no matter how institutionalized and

political hierarchy, both intra- and extraorganizational groups act as nodes for the exchange of information and influence. As an example, at the intraorganizational level, there are the coalitions and cliques which give a special flavor to the Congress. At the extraorganizational level are groups such as the top-level *ad hoc* unit assembled by President Kennedy in October 1962, at the time of the Cuban missile crisis. That group was called together because the President perceived that the usual organizational channels were inadequate in the face of the communication demands (information gathering, processing, and evaluation) imposed by the crisis.[6]

In modified form, the three propositions advanced about organizational channels apply also to group channels. That is, the groups of importance are not necessarily structurally part of the political system, their operation as political channels is frequently intermittent or partial, and the political uses to which they are put differ widely. Thus, for the purpose of analyzing the pattern of group channels in any system, few real complications are added by the distinction between organizations and groups.

However, in comparing entire systems the distinction becomes important, because, as we move from the more open to the more absolutist political format, we find fewer and fewer key political communication activities performed by groups, except at the very highest levels of decision. The types of political control and predictability sought by absolutist elites are rendered difficult if political communication is carried on in the less formal group channels. The elites prefer organizational or

---

formal they might be. Thus, to him the Supreme Court is a group whereas in our terminology it would be a small organization.

[6] In addition to the President, the group included among others Vice-President Lyndon Johnson, Robert Kennedy, Dean Rusk, Robert McNamara, and Douglas Dillon from the Cabinet, and others from the presidential staff, the State Department, the Central Intelligence Agency, and the Defense Department. For more detail on the group and its operation see Henry M. Pachter, *Collision Course: The Cuban Missile Crisis and Coexistence* (New York: Frederick A. Praeger, Inc., 1963), particularly pp. 11ff. See also Theodore C. Sorensen, *Decision-Making in the White House* (New York: Columbia University Press, 1963), *passim*.

mass media channels in which control and predictability are increased. This is not to claim that groups cease to exist; family, friendship, and intraorganizational groups remain. However, in absolutist systems there is an attempt to relieve such groups of much of their autonomous political communication. Sometimes group communication activities are suppressed, and at other times the activities are formalized to the point at which new organizational channels result. The new organizational channels at first glance may resemble collections of groups by virtue of the small scale of the operating unit or "cell"; but, because of the formalization of communication and the amount of control exercized, the new units are really small organizations. Both techniques of subordination of group life are illustrated by the recent history of Cuba. There reformist, family, and friendship groups have been stilled or coopted by the Castro regime while revolutionary *ad hoc* policy-making and policy-implementing groups have been transformed into bureaucracies with control over newly created organizational channels.

In sum, the mixture of organizational and group channels might well be a structural concomitant of political format. More specifically, it would seem that, where an open and competitive political system is in operation, group channels would proliferate. Where the more absolutist model is successfully in force, the political importance of group channels would diminish.

MASS MEDIA AS CHANNELS

As noted in the first chapter, a complex political system and its processes are very hard to observe at first hand. What most of us observe are *reports* of certain events and activities which in turn are only the behavioral outcroppings of political processes. For our reports of these events and activities we most frequently depend on the mass media or on others who themselves depend on the mass media.

Structural possibilities for a gigantic and bizarre hoax inhere in this situation. If it were possible to secure the conspiratorial cooperation of two thousand mass media personnel in key places, almost two hundred million Americans and a sizable part of the rest of the world could be led to believe that the President was dead or that atomic weapons were being used on Communist China.[7] Let the President in the flesh shout from the White House lawn that he was very much alive or deny at the top of his lungs that atomic bombs were being used on China, his messages would reach only the most limited audience as long as the conspiracy of the two thousand held. Only with the physical takeover of the national mass media by a centrally controlled agency with internal lines of communication, such as the Army, could the information tide sustaining the hoax be turned.

Though fanciful, the consequences of our imaginary conspiracy are instructive because they remind us how completely most citizens of developed societies depend on the mass media for primary information about the functioning of the national political system. This, of course, does not mean that the content of the media shapes political behavior in any direct and easily predictable manner, even in tightly controlled systems such as the Soviet. On the contrary, most current writing on the mass media and politics goes to some length to point out that the relationship between the two is very complex.[8] How-

[7] It is instructive to speculate on who should be included among the key two thousand personnel. Primarily they would be *gatekeepers* who in turn had the organizational resources needed to perpetrate the hoax on their own organizations, the wire services, radio, TV, and the newspapers.

As to the possibilities of social disorganization which inhere in the hoax, the famous Orson Welles radio broadcast "The War of the Worlds" in 1938 is instructive. Despite repeated warnings that the broadcast, describing an invasion by Martians, was fictional, thousands of listeners became panic stricken. Had the broadcast subject matter been more credible, had all stations carried the same broadcast, and had no warnings regarding its fictional nature been given, the chaos ensuing might well have brought national life to a standstill. See Hadley Cantril, *The Invasion from Mars* (Princeton, N.J.: Princeton University Press, 1940).

[8] See for instance V. O. Key, Jr., *Public Opinion and American Democracy* (New York: Alfred A. Knopf, 1961), particularly Chapters 14 and 15, and Robert E. Lane, *Political Life* (Glencoe, Illinois: The Free Press, 1959), particularly Chapter 19.

No attempt has been made here to give the reader a basic understanding

ever, the existence of national mass media, with all that they imply in increased message capacity, speed, and pervasiveness, changes in a basic way a system's potential for political communication. Structurally, the hoax suggested above would be just as easy to perpetrate in the Soviet Union as in the United States; in fact, because of Soviet centralization of media control, it might well be easier. In either case, under the conditions of the hoax, approximately 0.001 per cent of the citizens are so located in the mass media structures that they could very rapidly reshape some important political images held by the other 99.999 per cent of the population. This is a distinctly modern situation.

Thus, all varieties of political systems that are serviced by well-developed mass media networks also enjoy communication potentialities, for both control and coverage that are not shared by their media-poor relations no matter how extensive the latter's organizational and group channels might be.

To state this point in a slightly different fashion, the growth of mass media in a society alters in the most fundamental manner some aspects of politics. News travels farther and faster in a mass media system, and the "homogenization" and spread of public information is facilitated. Publicity assumes a new role, and a corps of specialists — reporters, columnists, editors, public information officers, and media personalities — is woven into the political process. The citizen participates politically as part of the media audience, tied to, and dependent upon, his newspaper, radio, and television set. But a word of caution is in order. It should not be assumed that the political trans-

---

of the mass media, their organization, operation, and relation to social life in general. For this purpose, several excellent books are available. For instance, for a basic introduction to the mass media in the United States, see Theodore Peterson, Jay W. Jensen, and William L. Rivers, *The Mass Media and Modern Society* (New York: Holt, Rinehart and Winston, Inc., 1965). For a very useful collection of essays and a good bibliography see Wilbur Schramm, ed., *Mass Communication* (Urbana: University of Illinois Press, 1960). A review of studies of mass media effects can be found in Joseph T. Klapper, *The Effects of Mass Communication* (Glencoe, Ill.: The Free Press, 1960), particularly Part One.

formation is complete, for personal contacts, face-to-face communication, and all sorts of nonmedia channels continue to be of vital importance in politics. If there is any single lesson taught by the results of several decades of research on communication processes, it is that the growth of the mass media results in a new mixture of mediated and nonmediated communication. The media do not simply displace or supersede other channels; rather, they link existing networks while giving rise to a host of dependent nets which service, disseminate, and frequently transform their product.

The structural picture of the mass media drawn so far suggests that we are dealing with long channels that somehow link informational centers or nodes with individuals and social groupings distant from the centers and from each other. There is some truth in this picture, but at best it is incomplete. For a more general comparative framework we have to consider at least two other types of mass media linkages:

1. *The Media as Lateral Channels.* Speaking of the role of prestige newspapers, such as *The New York Times* and the *Washington Post,* in foreign policy formation, Bernard Cohen notes that,

> By giving policy makers in both branches an insight into the political perceptions of men with important roles in the political process, the press helps to create common understandings or interpretations of political reality. There is thus some significance for the governmental — and hence public — debate on foreign policy in the fact that both Executive officials and Congressmen draw on approximately the same sources for their wider knowledge of "what is going on in the world," and how important it seems to be. Certain kinds of behavior can thus be reasonably predicted, and mutual expectation can become the basis for policy planning. Despite the specialized and confidential character of the State Department's diplomatic channels of information, continuous and meaningful discourse among foreign policy-making officials in all parts of the government, at all times and at all levels, is possible within the bounds set by this independent source of information and intellectual structuring of policy.[9]

[9] Bernard C. Cohen, *The Press and Foreign Policy* (Princeton, N.J.: Princeton University Press, 1963), p. 246.

Quite literally, important people in Washington and in other capitals around the world talk to each other through the mass media.

Such patterns may be equally prevalent in political systems in which there is otherwise minimal vertical media diffusion. Even in these systems, although there are few opportunities for grass-roots reading, listening, or viewing, the national elites clustered in the capital city have access to the mass media and use them for lateral political communication.

2. *The Media as Links in Other Chains.* In some of the developing countries, two types of persons are most likely to see a movie. The first is the urban dweller, participant in the modern economy at least to the extent that he pays cash to go to the commercial cinema in order to see "the latest." The second is the rural isolate, visited by some administrative arm of government such as community development and treated to an instructional film, frequently on some subject such as postnatal care or the construction of pit latrines. Here we have an example of an organizational channel using the mass media at the final stage as a "multiplier" of messages.

At times the ordering of the organizational and mass media linkages is reversed, as with farm radio forums and "tele-clubs," where the mass media are used for the initial dissemination of information and then structured local organizations continue the discussion and interpretation triggered by the media.[10] In both types of linkage it is noteworthy that mixtures of organizational and media channels are consciously established in order to achieve political goals. Students of communism have long realized how crucial to the operation of political systems such mixed channels can be, and students of political change and development are now acquiring the same awareness.[11]

[10] See J. C. Mathur and Paul Neurath, *An Indian Experiment in Farm Radio Forums* (Paris: UNESCO, 1959); Roger Louis and Joseph Rovan, *Television and Tele-clubs in Rural Communities,* Reports and Papers on Mass Communication, No. 16 (Paris: UNESCO, 1955); and UNESCO, *Rural Television in Japan* (Paris: UNESCO, 1960).

[11] See Ithiel de Sola Pool, "The Mass Media and Politics in the Modernization Process," in Lucian W. Pye, ed., *Communications and Political Development* (Princeton, N.J.: Princeton University Press, 1963).

Before leaving the mass media as channels, one final point should be made. The boundary problem discussed in the previous chapter is particularly acute when we attempt to decide *which* media activity has political consequences, that is, *when* media channels should be thought of as political communication channels.

The problem becomes more clearly drawn if we examine two types of occurrences. The first is well represented by the "great debates" of 1960 in which Kennedy and Nixon as presidential candidates confronted each other on television before an audience which averaged seventy-one million Americans. Both social scientists and political pundits agree that the debates were the most important single campaign episode serving to overcome Nixon's early lead in voter support.[12] Here the political system consequences of communication in media channels are about as clear-cut and direct as one could hope for in the complexity of dealing with macroeffects in a large national system.

However, consider a second type of example. Eisenstadt quotes an Israeli settler as saying,

> I always like to listen to the news and the radio. It is very important because only in this way can I feel that I know what happens in the State, that I am a real citizen.[13]

We know that the *aggregate* of media experiences like the one above can result in national political transformations of primary importance; but when citizen X listens to program Y it is impossible to link the system consequences to the event in any direct manner. The individual transformations sparked by this type of mediated communication develop for years before they affect the national political system. The consequences are im-

[12] See Sidney Kraus, ed., *The Great Debates* (Bloomington, Ind.: Indiana University Press, 1962) and Theodore H. White, *The Making of the President, 1960* (New York: Pocket Books, Inc., 1960), particularly Chapter 11. The estimate of audience size is from Frank Stanton, "A CBS View," in Kraus, *op. cit.*, p. 66.

[13] S. N. Eisenstadt, "Communication Systems and Social Structure: An Exploratory Comparative Study," *Public Opinion Quarterly*, Vol. XIX, No. 2, Summer 1955, p. 159.

portant, but they are often far removed from the subject matter and intent of the original communications.[14]

SPECIALIZED CHANNELS FOR INTEREST
ARTICULATION AND AGGREGATION

Consider two seemingly dissimilar acts: 1. An American housewife walks to her neighbor's basement on election day and casts her ballot for the presidential candidate of her choice. 2. Halfway around the world in Asia a militant leftist student joins a street demonstration and thirty minutes later is swept along in a chanting, rock-throwing attack on the American Embassy. For our purposes can these two behaviors be embedded in some common frame of meaning? Probably yes, for both the voter and the rioter are communicating choice or preference directly up some political hierarchy through special channels that do not fall easily into the typology of organizations, groups, or mass media developed above. This does not mean that organizations, groups, and the mass media do not shape the behavior of the voter and the rioter; of course they do, at least potentially. But the channels used for expression of preference are of an order different from those we have previously discussed.

These channels are used for the articulation and aggregation of interests only under special circumstances. The citizen cannot express himself through these channels whenever he feels the need, as he might on other occasions write a letter to the editor, speak at a union meeting, or complain to the bureaucracy. The social situation has to be "right." It must be election time, or the preconditions for mob action must be present. Thus, the channels are intermittent in operation and in a sense impermanent. In the case of well-institutionalized electoral procedures, the channels can be reconstituted on demand, but, once the communication tasks incident to the election are completed, the channels again cease to exist. In the case of the riot,

---

[14] David Riesman, among others, has discussed the mechanisms through which media-supported character transformations eventually give rise to a new style of politics. See his *The Lonely Crowd* (New Haven: Yale University Press, 1950), particularly Chapters IV and IX. This is a subject to which we shall return in Chapter VII.

the action forges its own channels, which disappear as the turmoil itself subsides.

The class of events that use or create such channels is not very well defined. The election and the riot seem to fit into the category, and perhaps the boycott and the public opinion poll should be included also. In any event, enough has been said to suggest that we are not dealing simply with a residual category with no common properties of its own. This brief discussion reminds us that in the study of organizations, groups, and the mass media we have not exhausted the possible communication components which the comparative analysis of political systems must note.

INTERACTION: AN EXAMPLE

As always happens with typologies, much of the richness of real life is lost, particularly when the subject matter is as luxuriant as ours. The communication networks which comprise the "nervous system" of a polity are intricate and complex in the extreme, as every student knows who has tried to trace and lay bare such networks. So, in the interest of ending this discussion on a more empirical note, let us return to the image of the fluoroscope with which the chapter began. Now, however, instead of looking in a general way at macrodifferences between national systems, let us confine our attention to one key "node" of a single national system. By so doing, some of the detail can be put back into the picture. In particular, let us focus on the mass media and political communication networks in Washington, D.C.[15] When the fluoroscope is turned on, what do we see?

[15] Aside from the intrinsic interest and importance of the example (the mass media and political communication in Washington), there are also pragmatic reasons for the choice. At least five books (of quite diverse quality) bear directly on some aspect of the problem. From earliest to most recently published they are Leo C. Rosten, *The Washington Correspondents* (New York: Harcourt, Brace & World, Inc., 1937), Douglass Cater, *The Fourth Branch of Government* (Boston: Houghton Mifflin Company, 1959), Bernard C. Cohen, *The Press and Foreign Policy* (Princeton, N.J.: Princeton University Press, 1963), Dan D. Nimmo, *Newsgathering in Washington* (New York: Atherton Press, 1964), William L. Rivers, *The Opinionmakers* (Boston: The Beacon Press, 1965). The discussion which follows is based on the composite picture which emerges from these five books.

At first glance, we might be struck by the number and diversity of organizations and individuals specializing in the production, gathering, processing, and dissemination of news and opinion about politics. The public information officers, press secretaries, public relations men, reporters, columnists, editors, and lesser operatives based in Washington must number in the thousands. Many work for the government, many others for the networks, news agencies, newspapers, and magazines, and still others are on commercial, personal, or foreign payrolls. Publicity, in the most general sense, is a very big and, at first glance, a very confusing business in Washington.

If we were to settle back and watch for awhile, certain patterns would emerge and begin to give order and predictability to the picture. We would notice that the specialists interact with each other in regular ways. Daily briefings are held to link official informational centers in the White House and the State Department with the reporters who cover those beats. Furthermore, through press conferences, top public officials on occasion make themselves available for direct interrogation, bypassing the information officers who normally stand between top officialdom and the working press. We would also notice that those who specialize in gathering news and purveying opinion evolve standardized search procedures, tailored to their informational needs. Through personal contacts, including contacts with other members of the working press, the political journalist cultivates the informal sources on which much of his work depends. Although it would not show up on our fluoroscope, these all-important formal and informal relationships are eased and maintained by a code of behavior, by certain conventions, confidences, unwritten agreements, niceties, and taboos which make it possible for the mass media specialists to live both with each other and with the various public officials on whom they report and depend.

There are other regularized and important patterns of communication in addition to the face-to-face exchanges just discussed. As suggested earlier, public officials use the mass media for a wide variety of purposes other than simply keeping themselves informed. To understand this second level of patterning we must look not only at the men who make and disseminate news and opinion, but also at the purposes served by the *products* which they turn out. The following list suggests some of the ways in which the mass media are used in political life in Washington.

1. *As an Index of What and Who Is Important, Newsworthy, or Politically Relevant.* It has been pointed out repeatedly that the political world does not order and arrange itself automatically; the media are largely responsible for this. When event X or problem Y appears as the lead article in *The New York Times,* then politicians, officials, and newsmen alike "know" that the event or problem is important. This is "information" of a special type. Prior to presenting information about events, the media tell busy men what events (and opinions) they should be paying attention to or, more precisely, what they *must* pay attention to if they wish to participate fully in political life.

2. *As a Tool for Gauging Public Opinion.* As Cater has pointed out,

> In an age of complex and fast-breaking events, the measurement of publicity comes to be taken as a cheap and convenient substitute for public opinion. For the politician and the bureaucrat the headline inch frequently serves as the day-to-day measure of public opinion on a great number of issues. By their responses to this synthetic public opinion they stimulate further publicity and so commences a reflexive cycle that has been known to move news stories from the inside to the front page and to reshape policies as surely as if public opinion had exerted its sovereign will.[16]

3. *As a Resource for Those with Plans, Problems, or Ambitions.* As the late Senator McCarthy demonstrated so convincingly, those who understand the newsmaking process can move themselves to the center of the political stage very quickly by self-generated publicity, even though as individuals they are not liked or trusted by the working press. Even those who are neither as unscrupulous nor as ambitious as the late senator view the press as a means for securing personal or bureaucratic advantage. The "trial balloon" — in which public reaction to

[16] Cater, *op. cit.,* pp. 12-13.

a proposed policy is tested before the policy is officially advocated — is a frequently employed, reputable political tactic. The news leak, the"off-the-record" briefing which removes a potential story from the public domain, and the calculated withholding or distortion of information are a few of the other tactics used by officials and their spokesmen in their continuing effort both to use and to disarm the press.

In sum, as soon as we look in detail at the web of communication networks active in any important node of a complex system, we realize that no simple typology will capture the richness of the relationships which characterize such a node. Individuals, groups, organizations, and the mass media are all linked together and all interact in the political process; and to equate idealized mass media patterns (a neutral press as watchdog of government) with the operative system is sadly to underestimate the complexity of the real world. In Washington, the mass media are in a real sense the fourth branch of government, not because they keep the other three branches "honest," but because they are the key structures in the public communication network on which functionaries in the other three branches depend. Were we able to gather data in any major capital of the world, most assuredly we would find a similarly complicated interplay and interdependence of communication specialists, public officials, and the mass media. Of course the interdependence would differ from country to country, as would mechanisms of media control, styles of newsgathering, modes of news presentation, and categories of media use. However, the complexity of networks would remain. Thus, although it is possible to reduce any network of political communication to a common set of structural building blocks, it is the total patterning of the network and the uses to which it is put which help us to understand politics. What factors determine the manner in which networks become patterned and used? Why does the process of political communication in Moscow or Cairo or even in London seem so different from political communication in Washington? Questions such as these are considered in the next chapter.

CHAPTER IV

The Determinants of
Communication Patterns and Use

IF A Russian-speaking American found himself in the Soviet Union, he would almost immediately be aware that he was in a different communication environment. As suggestive of differences in national style, consider the following lightly disguised radio conversation between an astronaut in his space craft and a national leader on the ground:

ASTRONAUT: We can hear you quite well. We report that the task of the —————— party and the —————— government is being fulfilled according to the set program. We feel excellent. Everything is in order.

NATIONAL LEADER: I could hear you quite well, ——————. I could follow everything. I am very happy that everything is fine with you and that you feel well. I wish you success. . . .

ASTRONAUT: We could hear you excellently. Once again be assured that we will fulfill the task of our homeland and our people.

NATIONAL LEADER: I'm very glad. I wish you good health. I'd like you to fulfill well the tasks which you received so as to glorify our homeland, our peoples, our party and the idea of —————— on the basis of which our state stands and on the basis of which we achieve all the things we have.

There is no mistaking that this is a Soviet dialogue, not an American one. The Astronaut is Vladimir Komarov and he is speaking to Premier Khrushchev on the occasion of the world's first multiman space flight.[1] Upon picking up *Pravda* our traveler would be struck by the manner in which it differed in content, style, and purpose from *The New York Times*. He would also find Soviet television quite unlike its American counterpart. If he remained in Moscow during an election, he would observe none of the ballyhoo, none of the fuss, and none of the contention which characterize an American election. In short, he would find no electoral campaign as it is traditionally conceived in the United States.

The longer our American traveler stayed in the Soviet Union and the more fully he became integrated into the society, the more aware he would become of differences in the communication environment. He would soon realize that controversies about freedom of expression focus on different objects and are carried on within different ideological and institutional frameworks in the two countries. Similarly he would frequently be reminded that the channels through which demands might be communicated to national elites — and the nature of the demands themselves — differ in the Soviet Union and the United States.

To attribute these and other differences to the fact that the Soviet Union is Communist and the United States a Western democracy is only a partial explanation. The differences in political format explain some but not all of the differences in political communication.

Think for a moment about Communist China. Suppose that our American tourist also knew Chinese and one day found himself in Peking. What differences in the communication environment would he notice as he moved from Soviet Communism to Chinese Communism?

First, he would notice changes in the content and style of

[1] As reported in *The New York Times*, October 13, 1964, p. 18. A most useful comparative work in this area is Wilbur Schramm, ed., *One Day in the World's Press* (Stanford, Calif.: Stanford University Press, 1959). The day referred to in the title is November 2, 1956, chosen because both the Hungarian Revolution and the Suez crisis were in process. Fourteen important world newspapers are translated and presented in facsimile reproductions in the volume.

mass media communication. These differences could be indexed by a comparison of *Pravda* and *Jen Min Jih Pao,* the largest Chinese daily newspaper. Soviet devils and problems are not necessarily Chinese devils and problems, nor are the methods used to exorcise the respective devils necessarily similar. Furthermore, he would notice different mixes of channels and even some new channels in operation in China. There our tourist would find posters (*tatzepao*) and many other devices used extensively for mass education and persuasion, with even the traditional opera transformed into a channel for political communication. Given the much less developed mass media system, he would find a greater predominance of mass organizations engaged in inculcating and maintaining "correct" revolutionary élan. In short, he would experience the communication environment generated when an underdeveloped society, lacking originally in long channels and media facilities, embarks on an ambitious program of social control and change under Marxist-Leninist leadership.[2] The Chinese patterns bear the imprint of Chinese culture, leadership, and lack of material and social resources. Marxism-Leninism is not sufficient to subordinate the differences brought about by these other influences.

Is there a way to systematize what we have been talking about up to this point? We want to know *where to look* in order to answer questions such as the following: Why are the mass media used extensively for political communication in some countries and not in others? Why do some elites build specialized organizational channels to serve as vertical links between themselves and their subjects? Why do political systems differ in the channels used to handle communication up the hierarchy during the policy-making and policy-implementing processes? Such questions could be multiplied endlessly, but our purpose here is neither to ask all the questions nor to suggest specific answers. Rather, we are interested in what

[2] For book-length discussions of political communication in Communist China see Franklin W. Houn, *To Change a Nation* (New York: The Free Press of Glencoe, Inc., 1961) and Frederick T. C. Yu, *Mass Persuasion in Communist China* (New York: Frederick A. Praeger, Inc., 1964).

types of factors affect the manner in which political communication channels are patterned and used. The previous chapter introduced the elements of the patterns, now we are concerned with the ways in which elements are put together in an operative system.

As implied in our example of the tourist traveling from the United States to the Soviet Union and then to Communist China, we need to be concerned with at least four classes of variables that bear on the determination of channel patterning and use. In shorthand form these are (1) economic, (2) sociocultural, (3) political, and (4) historical factors. Each will be explicated in turn.

ECONOMIC FACTORS

All political communication takes place within limits set by the nation's general level of economic development. This is most obvious with respect to the mass media. Thus, as much as the Communist Chinese elites might wish to have a national television network at their disposal for political purposes, at the present stage of Chinese economic development this is a clear impossibility. If nothing else, rural electrification has not progressed to the point at which TV receivers, even if they were available, could be operated on a national scale. Of course it is not only electrification but also lack of productive capacity, transport capacity, and media expertise that inhibit the spread of television. Similarly, economic limits are imposed on the diffusion of the other media, even though the particular factors differ as we move from country to country or from electronics to print.

Consider some of the financial problems faced by a publisher attempting to start a small daily newspaper in an Indian vernacular language. Even if initial capitalization of $7,500 to $15,000 is available,

> . . . that only begins to solve the problems.
> The English-language newspapers with prestige receive a major share of government and private advertising budgets. . . . Only a small amount trickles down to the Indian-language papers trying to serve the smaller cities. Because of this, the smaller papers

have to charge higher advertising rates in an effort to survive. This makes their advertising still less attractive to purchasers.

Newsprint costs more outside the great cities. . . .

News agency costs are proportionally higher on a small daily, and, if it is a local-language daily, the cost of translation must be added to the fee for the wire service. . . .

. . . even the wastepaper value of a newspaper is something that purchasers or subscribers take into account. They can subtract from the price of the paper the money they receive from selling the used copy. . . . The less advertising it has, the fewer pages it can print, and the less it will be worth as wastepaper to the subscribers.[3]

Here we have chosen an example involving a medium and a set of economic rules which differ from those used in the Chinese example. But even the Chinese leadership would experience economic problems in establishing a local daily, for newsprint and presses are scarce commodities north of the Himalayas too.

If we leave specific examples and turn to aggregate data on the national level, we find, as might be expected, that the level of mass media development and the level of economic development are closely related. The strength of this relationship is suggested in Table IV-1, in which four indices of national mass media development are correlated with an index of national economic development. The upper figure in each row of the table is the product-moment correlation coefficient, and the lower, in parentheses, is the number of cases (nations) on which the correlation is based.[4]

---

3 Wilbur Schramm, *Mass Media and National Development* (Stanford, Calif.: Stanford University Press, 1964), p. 103.

4 For those not familiar with the statistic in question, the product-moment correlation coefficient is a measure of the strength of the relationship between two variables. The coefficient associated with a perfect linear relationship would be 1.00 (or −1.00). The coefficient indicating no relationship between the two variables would be 0. As a naïve example of a perfect relationship, imagine a group of 100 children each of whom weighs exactly two pounds for every inch of height. In this case the product-moment correlation coefficient between height and weight would be 1.00. In any "real" group of 100 children there would of course be some positive relation between height and weight, but it would not be perfect. That is, the prod-

TABLE IV.1   *The Relationship between Level of Economic Development and Level of Mass Media Development*

	Gross national product per capita
Daily newspaper circulation per 1,000 population	.80 (111)
Radio receivers per 1,000 population	.85 (107)
Television sets per 1,000 population	.75 (69)
Cinema attendance per capita	.65 (100)

Source: Constructed from data in Bruce M. Russett, et. al., *World Hand-book of Political and Social Indicators* (New Haven: Yale University Press, 1964), pp. 272, 274-75.

Two points should be emphasized. First, the table tells us nothing about the political uses to which mass media capacity is put; it reminds us only that economically advanced nations tend to have well developed mass media systems and that the reverse is also true. The manner in which these facilities are used or not used for political communication is another matter. Second, the relationships presented, although strong statistically, are by no means perfect. Thus, we will find deviant cases — less developed states, for instance, with television systems burgeoning out of proportion to what one would expect on the basis of economic predictors alone. Cuba, for example, in 1961 ranked thirteenth in the world in television receivers per one thousand population, ahead of countries such as France and Switzerland. Yet Cuban gross national product per capita ranked only thirty-second in the world and in dollar value amounted to less than one-third the GNP per capita of

uct-moment correlation would be greater than 0 but less than 1.00. For a more precise explanation see any standard text on statistics, for example Hubert M. Blalock, *Social Statistics* (New York: McGraw-Hill Book Company, 1960), pp. 285ff.

Switzerland and less than one-half that of France.[5] The causes and consequences of such patterns of media growth and deviance will be explored in Chapter VII.

Economic factors also affect the patterning and use of organizational and group channels. These relationships are harder to characterize and quantify, for they stem from the larger interaction between economic development (or industrialization) and types of social organization. The work of Max Weber and Talcott Parsons is relevant here. As an example, F. X. Sutton, writing in this tradition, has characterized two types of societies.

> An "agricultural" society has the following essential characteristics:
>
> 1. Predominance of ascriptive, particularistic, diffuse patterns.
> 2. Stable local groups and limited spatial mobility.
> 3. Relatively simple and stable "occupational" differentiation.
> 4. A "deferential" stratification system of diffuse impact. . . .
>
> As essential sociological features of a *modern industrial society* I suggest the following:
>
> 1. Predominance of universalistic, specific, and achievement norms.
> 2. High degree of social mobility (in a general — not necessarily "vertical" — sense.)
> 3. Well-developed occupational system, insulated from other social structures.
> 4. "Egalitarian" class system based on generalized patterns of occupational achievement.
> 5. Prevalence of "associations," i.e., functionally specific, non-ascriptive structures.[6]

This is not an easy typology to digest if swallowed in one gulp. But in essence, the lesson to be drawn is that societies which differ in their economic bases differ also in systematic

[5] Data from Bruce R. Russett, et al., *World Handbook of Political and Social Indicators* (New Haven: Yale University Press, 1964), pp. 126 and 155.

[6] F. X. Sutton, "Social Theory and Comparative Politics," in Harry Eckstein and David E. Apter, eds., *Comparative Politics* (New York: The Free Press of Glencoe, Inc., 1963), p. 71; emphasis in original.

ways with respect to social structure, social mobility, norms, and predominant types of social organization. Our claim is that political communication in group and organizational channels is in turn affected by these economic-sociological transformations. For instance, consider the implications of Sutton's fifth point under *modern industrial society*. One can suggest on the basis of his formulation that since nonascriptive organizations and groups are more likely to be found in industrial societies, they are also more likely to be found operating as channels of political communication. Some support for this hypothesis comes from the work of Banks and Textor who suggest (on the basis of empirical materials) that "Polities where interest articulation by associational groups is significant or moderate [as opposed to limited or negligible], tend to be those whose per capita gross national product is [either] very high or high." [7]

Whether this hypothesis would stand up under rigorous scrutiny is not of immediate concern to us. It is important to realize that the patterning and operation of group and organizational channels in a society are affected by economic factors in at least two ways. First, the material and social technology (mimeograph machines, telephones, the postal service) which an advanced economy puts at the service of groups and organizations enhances their communication capabilities in obvious ways. Second, the sociological transformations that occur as the economic bases of a society change make possible and probable the emergence of new organizational and group channels, or at least channels of a different sort. Sutton's typology sensitizes us to this second point. Furthermore, it calls into question our

[7]Arthur S. Banks and Robert B. Textor, *A Cross-Polity Survey* (Cambridge, Mass.: MIT Press, 1963), "finished characteristics" 116 and 35. The Banks and Textor volume is an experimental effort, the bulk of which "consists of computer 'printout.' This is material printed by a 7090 computer in the form of grammatical English-language sentences, which are grouped by subject into paragraphs." (p. 1). The printout section is not paginated but is indexed according to the variables or "finished characteristics" presented on the page. Although the effort is open to both substantive and methodological criticism, there is much in the volume of interest to students of political communication, for many of the variables considered are, in our framework, communication variables.

tidy analytical distinction between economic and social factors as determinants of patterns of political communication. At the least, it should be clear that as soon as we ask serious questions about economic determinants, we are forced to a more thorough consideration of social factors.

SOCIOCULTURAL FACTORS

The articulation of political channels is affected by three types of sociocultural factors. Here we label these *skills, norms,* and *institutions*.[8]

Skills. Literacy is the most obvious social skill affecting political communication, but there is a host of derivative vocational skills such as printing and journalism which are also important. The development of literacy and its relationship to communication and political change will be treated in more detail in Chapter VII. It is sufficient now to suggest that at the national level, literacy — considered as an index of sociocultural development — bears a strong relationship to the mass media and to the economic development indices used earlier in Table IV.1.

The upper figure in each row of Table IV.2 is the product-moment correlation coefficient and the lower, in parentheses, is the number of cases (nations) on which the correlation is based. Also, the earlier cautions apply about deviant cases and the danger of making inferences from communication capacity to communication use.

Norms. In a discussion of administration in Thailand, James Mosel makes the following telling comparison:

> In the bureaucracies of the West the official is often described as having a dual allegiance: to the rationality of regulations on one hand, and to his superior on the other. This duality frequently gives rise to administrative conflicts and provides the official with a basis for defying his superior. In the Thai bureaucracy alle-

[8] As a fourth category we could add what might be called sociogeographical *diversities*. Examples are the linguistic, ethnic, and topographic differences which set internal limits on all types of social communication in many national environments. The discussion of such bases of communication discontinuity will be postponed until Chapter VI, where it more properly fits.

TABLE IV.2   *The Relationship between Level of Literacy and Levels of Mass Media and Economic Development*

	Literacy (percentage of population age 15 and over literate)
Daily newspaper circulation per 1,000 population	.88 (111)
Radio receivers per 1,000 population	.80 (107)
Television sets per 1,000 population	.69 (68)
Cinema attendance per capita	.71 (99)
Gross national product per capita	.80 (117)

Source: Constructed from data in Russett, op. cit., p. 283

giance is much more one-sided, and conflicts of this kind are less likely to occur. . . . In Thailand the government employee has always been a "King's servant" (kharachakarn), not a "public servant." . . . the vertical orientation favors a one-way communication system — downward.[9]

Here we have an example of the manner in which long-standing, culturally anchored patterns of behavior affect the operation of political channels, opening up some and closing off others. Similarly, without attempting to be too precise, we can see clearly that social "egalitarianism" affects political communication in the United States in a variety of ways. Few observers of the American scene, from Tocqueville to the present, have failed to comment on this theme. The American mythology that any man's son can become President has as its less mythological communication corollary the proposition that the President and many lesser lights should be accessible to the publics they purport to serve. Spectacles such as the Presiden-

[9] James N. Mosel, "Thai Administrative Behavior," in William J. Siffin, ed., *Toward the Comparative Study of Public Administration* (Bloomington, Ind.: Indiana University Press, 1959), pp. 322-23.

tial news conference are rooted as much in the egalitarianism of American public life as they are in the desire of the executive to inform and mold public attitudes. Direct channels, from executive to the people and from the people to the executive, are not nearly so common in European societies with more aristocratic traditions.

Institutions. Just as societies differ in the availability of communication skills and the impact of norms on the patterning of channels, so they differ also in the social institutions potentially available for use in political communication. At the beginning of the chapter it was mentioned that the Chinese leadership uses the traditional opera as a channel for political education and socialization. Institutions of this sort, commanding a significant audience or clientele and having high authority, are used at times for political communication by regimes covering a broad political spectrum.

U Nu's campaign strategy in the 1960 election in Burma offers an example. Nu first announced that if elected he would make Buddhism the state religion. Since about six out of seven Burmese are at least nominally Buddhist, this promise had widespread (potential) appeal. Next, just before the campaign officially began, Nu entered a monastery to spend six weeks as a monk. He then embarked on an extensive campaign of speechmaking in rural areas.

> Wherever U Nu went . . . he called on the Buddhist monks and the village elders, gave them his respects, and offered food and alms. Often his speeches were only Buddhist sermons, but to the people they rang clearer and carried more meaning than speeches on socialism. . . . Monks canvassed for U Nu in the villages, threatening to leave the villagers if they did not vote for him.[10]

As clues to the voters, the ballot boxes of Nu's party were painted Buddhist yellow and adorned with a picture of the leader.

> Old women who had never voted in their lives, dragged themselves to the polling booths to vote for him, and some were found

[10] Maung Maung, "New Parliament in Burma," *India Quarterly*, Vol. XVI, No. 2, April-June 1960, pp. 142-43.

in the booths doing homage to his picture as if he were Buddha himself.[11]

Nu's faction won the election by an unexpectedly large margin. Although it is impossible to attach direct causal importance to any one aspect of the campaign, Nu, by exploiting existing religious channels and symbolism, undoubtedly was able to link himself more immediately and enduringly to certain segments of the population than would otherwise have been the case.

POLITICAL FACTORS

No one who is familiar with the modern world has to be told that patterns of political communication differ greatly in ways directly attributable to differences in political organization and ideology. Our tourist friend, introduced at the beginning of this chapter, found that in the Soviet Union the ownership, content, and functions of the mass media bear little resemblance to their counterparts in the United States. He found also that dissidents had to seek out different channels of complaint and criticism and at times had to be silent altogether. On experiencing a Soviet election, he realized that the communication activities related to the event were of a lesser scale and for a different purpose than in the American case. All these differences, and many more, are attributable to the different political formats under which the United States and the Soviet Union operate. For the present analysis, these communication differences can be thought of as independent of variations in economic and sociocultural factors.[12]

[11] Ibid, p. 143. See also Richard Butwell and Fred von der Mehden, "The 1960 Election in Burma," *Pacific Affairs,* Vol. XXXIII, No. 2, June 1960, pp. 144-57; and Fred von der Mehden, "The Changing Pattern of Religion and Politics in Burma," in Robert K. Sakai, ed., *Studies on Asia 1961* (Lincoln, Neb.: University of Nebraska Press, 1961).

[12] Although slightly out of date, the best brief introduction to the mass communication correlates of the different political formats in the United States and the Soviet Union is Fred S. Siebert, Theodore Peterson, and Wilbur Schramm, *Four Theories of the Press* (Urbana, Ill.: University of Illinois Press, 1956), reissued as a paperback in 1963. The four theories treated are the authoritarian, the libertarian, the social responsibility, and the Soviet communist.

It is possible to take almost any two polities, even two communist systems, and draw out in this manner differences in their patterns of political communication. But comparative politics currently proceeds on the assumption that higher levels of abstraction are needed, that we must compare types of systems, not just individual systems. Thus, the last decade has witnessed a proliferation of classificatory schemes. The taxonomic effort is not new; as is so often the case, it goes back at least to Aristotle.[13] What *is* distinctly new is the volume and seeming heterogeneity of the effort. The rule in current practice seems to be, "every man his own taxonomist."

For our purposes, the interesting aspect of the explosion in classifications is that one can draw out of each of the individual efforts a set of propositions about the patterning of political communication which underlies the type. In short, either explicit or implicit in each box of every taxonomy is a model or representation of a system of political communication. When the taxonomies are viewed in this way, much of the initial heterogeneity disappears, for all of them in one manner or another differentiate systems according to the degree of communication competition and freedom allowed or encouraged. This is another way of saying that every taxonomy bears in some manner on the second question posed initially in Chapter I: Who should be able to say what, in which channels, to whom, for what purposes? In order to discriminate between political systems, all taxonomists seem to ask what communication "rights" are given to various groups or individual participants in the political process. Once this question is answered, patterns of political communication are thrown into relief and characterization of the patterns themselves often becomes a parsimonious way of indexing differences between systems.

The procedure is clear when we are dealing with familiar types such as the Western democratic and the Soviet totalitarian models. As we saw in Chapter II, as soon as the political

---

13 See Robert A. Dahl, *Modern Political Analysis* (Englewood Cliffs, N.J.: Prentice-Hall, Inc., 1963), Chapter Four. For a taxonomy of the taxonomists and a good recent bibliography see Robert A. Packenham, "Approaches to the Study of Political Development," *World Politics,* Vol. XVII, No. 1, October 1964, pp. 108-120.

format is named, certain patterns of political communication can be predicted. In this case the democratic format is clearly associated with political communication patterns that are more competitive and less controlled than the totalitarian. But even in less familiar typologies the same dimensions and distinctions can be found.

As an example, consider the "mobilization" and "consociational" types developed by Apter and Rosberg to deal with contemporary African political systems.[14] In their formulation, the mobilization system is characterized by hierarchic authority, a demand for total allegiance from those who participate, tactical flexibility on the part of the political elite, and organizational unitarism with subordinate groups being direct affiliates of leadership structures. On the other hand, the consociational system is characterized by pyramidal authority with constituent units having some autonomy, tolerance of multiple loyalties among those who participate, and a feeling that compromise is necessary since organizational subgroups are participating voluntarily. Even on basis of such a brief sketch, one could predict that political communication in the mobilization system would be less competitive and more carefully controlled by the ruling elite than in the consociational system. Certain channels such as an opposition press, which might exist in the latter type of system, would probably be missing in the former. Other channels such as the highly politicized trade union are more likely to be found in the former.

In sum, it is not surprising to find that the patterning of political communication in a society depends directly on the political "rules of the game" which characterize the system. The very concept of political authoritarianism, in all its various guises both ancient and modern, implies some limiting of

[14] David E. Apter and Carl G. Rosberg, "Nationalism and Models of Political Change in Africa," in Donald P. Ray, ed., *The Political Economy of Contemporary Africa* (Washington, D.C.: The National Institute of Social and Behavioral Science, 1959). Apter subsequently presented a modified version of the typology in which the concept of "consociational" system was replaced with "reconciliation" system. See David E. Apter, "Political Religion in the New Nations," in Clifford Geertz, ed., *Old Societies and New States* (New York: The Free Press of Glencoe, Inc., 1963).

the scope of communication. In all political systems that we think of as authoritarian there are always channels, both horizontal and vertical, which are purposely closed to certain groups, individuals, and types of content. Similarly, in those political formats which we consider more democratic, there always exist certain configurations of channels designed to facilitate or protect the communication activities of "oppositions" of various sorts. The mix of channel "openness" and "closedness" in any real system is so complex that it is difficult to characterize in unilinear fashion. But it is a tribute to both the wisdom of the elders of political theory and the obduracy of political problems that we continue to differentiate systems according to the patterns of political communication which result from the structuring of power.

HISTORICAL FACTORS

Under this heading we group those determinants of communication patterns which derive from particular experiences or attributes of the society not systematically related to the economic, sociocultural, or political factors discussed above.

In his study of Burmese politics, Lucian Pye gives an example of such a historical determinant — in this case actually a *set* of determinants.[15] Under British rule, Pye says, there grew up among the Burmese administrative class self-identifications and organizational procedures poorly suited to effective performance in the postcolonial world. Similarly, among Burmese politicians, common participation in agitational and conspiratorial political action against the British and the Japanese formed a political style not well suited to national development under conditions of self-rule. Thus the administrator, unclear about the difference between ritual and rationality and ambivalent about the nature of progress and modernization, has great difficulty communicating informally with his coworkers in the implementation of policy. Also the politician, not sure of what his role should be in an independent Burma and not always positive that he actually deserves high office,

[15] See Lucian W. Pye, *Politics, Personality, and Nation Building* (New Haven, Conn.: Yale University Press, 1962), particularly Part Five.

insulates himself from constituents and divorces himself from causes that might prove unpopular. As a result, patterns of communication within the bureaucracy, between the political elite and the masses, and between the politicians and the administrators are all affected.

No claim is made here that the organizational and psychological legacy left by the colonial experience is completely responsible for the observed peculiarities of existing patterns of political communication. Pye himself discusses a wide range of possible influences stemming from Burmese culture, institutions, and personality. Rather, the point is simply that, had the Burmese system not undergone the colonial experience, patterns of political communication would be palpably different today.[16]

Without entering into the classic debate about whether heroes make history or history makes heroes, we must also consider the impact of certain leadership styles on political communication. Fidel Castro illustrates the point well. In the first years after his assumption of power in Cuba he was constantly before the microphones and television cameras, explaining, exhorting, and accusing. It is difficult accurately to assess the political impact of his hundreds of hours of speechmaking, but both friends and foes of the regime agree that his visual and verbal presence were, and still are, central to the Revolution. Castro did not create the mass media channels which he used in order to widen and continue the bases of his charismatic relationship with the Cuban masses.[17] Rather, he exploited existing facilities and in time built new organizational

[16] For more general material on the colonial experience, see Rupert Emerson, *From Empire to Nation* (Cambridge, Mass.: Harvard University Press, 1960), particularly Part Three. Also relevant is O. Mannoni, *Prospero and Caliban* (New York: Frederick A. Praeger, Inc., 1964); this was first published in 1950 under the title *Psychologie de la Colonisation*. Arthur S. Banks and Robert B. Textor, in *A Cross-Polity Survey* (Cambridge, Mass.: The MIT Press, 1963) also present propositions on the differential impact of types of colonial rule.

[17] See Richard R. Fagen, "Charismatic Authority and the Leadership of Fidel Castro," *Western Political Quarterly*, Vol. XVIII, No. 2, June 1965, pp. 275-84.

channels appropriate for his leadership style and evolving ideology. In the first instance it was Castro himself, rather than existing economic, sociocultural, or political factors, who most directly influenced the patterning and use of vertical channels of political communication in Cuba. This much, at least, Castro has in common with Hitler and Franklin D. Roosevelt. All three at first exploited existing vertical channels in their systems in new ways consonant with their innovative leadership styles. Only later did the political format change in each case, providing new organizational and media channels specifically keyed to the communication styles and needs of the leaders.

Detailed study of the communication patterns of any polity would always reveal a range of determinants of the sort suggested here. Innovative personalities, technological breakthroughs, social upheavals and dislocations, and foreign influence and domination all affect the patterning of political communication. To disentangle the web of causality in any particular case may not be so important as to remain sensitive to the multiplicity of factors which might be operative and which thus might be listed under this fourth category.

As can be seen, we have treated historical factors as a residual. Differences in communication patterns not attributable in some systematic way to economic, sociocultural, and political factors are grouped under the historical label, and there is at least a hint that these materials lend themselves less well to comparative analysis. But this need not be the case. Such factors as the legacies of colonial experience and the communication consequences of various leadership styles can also be characterized and treated within some comparative framework. As always, much work remains to be done, and the few paragraphs devoted to historical factors here do not begin to suggest the possibilities for systematic analysis in this area.[18]

[18] For a stocktaking by historians which includes much soul searching and many useful ideas, see the symposium edited by Louis Gottschalk, *Generalization in the Writing of History* (Chicago: University of Chicago Press, 1963).

CHAPTER V

Political Images:
Distributions and Flows

IN THE last two chapters, we have focused on channels of political communication and the various factors that might affect the manner in which these channels are patterned and used. We have paid little attention to the end product of the communication process: the political images held by individuals. It is time to rectify this deficiency.

Before doing so, it is necessary to remove some of the ambiguity which frequently surrounds the use of the concept of "image." As employed here, an image is a cognitive attribute of an individual. It may be a memory or recollection of a past occurrence, a belief about what will occur in the future, a "fact" such as "two times two equals four," an opinion or attitude relating to any conceivable subject matter, or some amalgam of memory, belief, fact, and opinion. Obviously, the cognitive environment of any given individual is made up of thousands and even millions of such images, more or less manifest, more or less strongly held, and more or less organized into coherent congeries and categories. Our purpose, however, is not the investigation of the cognitive environments of individuals, but rather the mapping of cognitive attributes (beliefs, attitudes, information, preferences, here generically called images) onto social and political variables. We are interested in who knows and believes what, how they came to know and believe what they do, and what difference all of this makes for the functioning of the political system. For these purposes, the concept of image serves as a shorthand way of referring to the entire class of cognitive attributes which must be considered in the study of individual political psychology as it relates to system functioning.

It is in this area that the study of political communication and the study of political behavior touch most intimately, for all of our political acts are bounded by the images of political reality or "pictures in our heads" which we carry about with us. No one has argued this more cogently than Walter Lippmann, who opened his classic book, *Public Opinion,* with the following paragraph:

> There is an island in the ocean where in 1914 a few Englishmen, Frenchmen, and Germans lived. No cable reaches that island, and the British mail steamer comes but once in sixty days. In September it had not yet come, and the islanders were still talking about the latest newspaper which told about the approaching trial of Madame Caillaux for the shooting of Gaston Calmette. It was, therefore, with more than usual eagerness that the whole colony assembled at the quay on a day in mid-September to hear from the captain what the verdict had been. They learned that for over six weeks now those of them who were English and those of them who were French had been fighting in behalf of the sanctity of treaties against those of them who were Germans. For six strange weeks they had acted as if they were friends, when in fact they were enemies.[1]

It is one thing to pay homage to the importance of the relationship between political images and political action and quite another to attempt to specify the mechanisms by which cognitions actually affect behavior and behaviors affect cognitions. The theoretical and empirical richness of this area of inquiry is very great. Much of what is currently labeled "be-

[1] Walter Lippmann, *Public Opinion* (New York: The Macmillan Company, 1954), p. 3. The first chapter of Lippmann's book is titled "The World Outside and the Pictures in Our Heads."

havioral research" involves an effort to analyze the interdependence of cognitive and behavioral patterns as they affect the political system.

Our sole purpose in this chapter, however, is to take a first look at political images, their component parts, and the ways in which they become distributed through social and political systems. Not to limit ourselves in this fashion would involve us in a book-length digression. In other words, we shall not concern ourselves in full measure with the cognitive bases of political behavior, fascinating and important as this subject is for the understanding of political life.

POLITICAL INFORMATION AND POLITICAL EVALUATION

Whenever we look in detail at a society, we find vast differences in the political information that conditions the operative reality of individuals. Thus in New Delhi sit Indian politicians who can characterize the workings of the Congress Party with utmost skill and consummate command of the facts; while

> In Bhoola, a Bhil village in Sirohi district, the villagers admit: "Yes, we have heard of the Congress. We have heard of the Congress; yes. Everyone talks of it."
>
> "But," pauses Kania, gravely puckering his bushy eyebrows, "but now that you mention it, we do not know whether Congress is a man or woman." [2]

As the public opinion polls constantly remind us, we need not confine our examples of the differential distribution of political information to the less developed countries. Thus Lane and Sears present the following familiar, but nevertheless instructive, data on American civic ignorance.[3]

[2] Kusum Nair, *Blossoms in the Dust* (New York: Frederick A. Praeger, Inc., 1962), p. 125.

[3] Reordered from data presented in Robert E. Lane and David O. Sears, *Public Opinion* (Englewood Cliffs, N.J.: Prentice-Hall, Inc., 1964), p. 61. The polls from which the data were originally taken are cited in Lane and Sears. See also V. O. Key, Jr., *Public Opinion and American Democracy* (New York: Alfred A. Knopf, Inc., 1961), Part I.

Question	Correct answers, national sample of the United States
Will you tell me what the three branches of the Federal Government are called?	19%
What do you know about the Bill of Rights? Do you know anything it says?	21%
What is meant by the electoral college?	35%
How many senators are there in Washington from your state?	55%
Will you tell me what the term "veto" means to you? For example, what does it mean when the President vetoes a bill sent him by Congress?	80%

All systems are characterized by rapid attenuation of political information as one moves from the centers of knowledge and power to the periphery. The data above characterize the end product of attenuation, and the patterning, as one scans the society, is in part predictable. For example, persons of low income, little education, and geographic isolation on the average always know much less about the system than their wealthier, better educated, and less isolated fellow citizens. In some systems the attenuation sets in very quickly as one moves through the social structure; perhaps only 10 per cent of the population can name the major political parties, whereas in other systems the figure would jump to 90 per cent. But always the attenuation occurs.[4]

Similarly, we could document horizontal patterns of attenuation of political information in all systems. This unevenness of informational distribution takes place for two reasons. The

[4] For a good discussion of informational attenuation and the factors which influence it see Wilbur Schramm, *Mass Media and National Development* (Stanford, Calif.: Stanford University Press, 1964), Chapter Two.

first is that with the division of labor always comes division of information. The busy congressman or general simply cannot command the specialized information that the Supreme Court Justice or Secretary of Agriculture does. Nor, obviously, can the Justice master the specialized information relevant to performing the congressional role. When there is agreement on the need for more similarity between the informational universes of two governmental structures or two individuals, special devices such as the briefing, the hearing, the joint committee, or the cocktail party are used. In the second place, members of all structures participate at times in the planned withholding of information. Sometimes the justification is security (as with the CIA) and sometimes political advantage is the prime motivation (as with competitive factions or cliques). In either case the impact on the lateral distribution of information is similar.

In talking about the vertical and horizontal distributions of political information, we have been avoiding two important problems. The first involves the question of consequences. It is one thing to map the distribution of political information in a system, and it is something else to say what the distribution means for the system's functioning — what political consequences the distribution has. It is probably of consequence for the system if 30 per cent of the adults are unaware that the nation exists and that they, as citizens, have the right to vote in national elections. But what if 90 per cent of the population cannot name the members of the Supreme Court? Does this disclose a significant characteristic of the system? Explication of this complicated problem area will be postponed until the next chapter.

There is a second more immediate problem. We began this chapter by talking about political images or "pictures in our heads" and rapidly switched to a discussion of political information. This simplication was designed to facilitate the introduction of the notion of distributions through the social and political structure. Information (and misinformation) are not the only, or necessarily even the most important, components of political images. There are also evaluational components. As Boulding reminds us in his more general discussion,

The subjective knowledge structure or image of any individual or organization consists not only of images of "fact" but also images of "value." . . . it is clear that there is a certain difference between the image which I have of physical objects in space and time and the valuations which I put on these objects or on the events which concern them. It is clear that there is a certain difference between, shall we say, my image of Stanford University existing at a certain point in space and time, and my image of the value of Stanford University. If I say "Stanford University is in California," this is rather different from the statement "Stanford University is a good university, or is a better university than X, or a worse university than Y." [5]

In reality, of course, it is usually very difficult to classify an actual political image as either information or evaluation. "The Democrats won the last election" is clearly information. "I hate the Democrats," is clearly evaluation. But what about, "The Democrats are undermining NATO"? At the least, this image has three interwoven themes: (1) The Democrats are doing X, Y, and Z (information or misinformation); (2) X, Y, and Z lead to a weakening of the NATO alliance (information or misinformation); (3) A weakening of NATO is bad (evaluation, communicated by the verb "undermine"). Most political images are of this sort: a complex amalgam of information and evaluation. Man is an evaluating animal and political man particularly so. Our introduction to political images is incom-

[5] Kenneth E. Boulding, *The Image* (Ann Arbor, Mich.: University of Michigan Press, 1956), p. 11. The dichotomization also handles images of the future. The statement "Stanford will double its enrollment in 40 years" is a prediction of "conditions to be" and can be considered a subtype of information or misinformation. On the other hand, the statement, "It would be very unfortunate if Stanford were to allow its enrollment to double," implies a preferred future condition and can be considered a subtype of evaluation. A similar formulation is found in Lasswell's distinction between *expectations* (which characterize a future state of affairs) and *demands* (which express a valuation or preference). See Harold D. Lasswell and Abraham Kaplan, *Power and Society* (New Haven, Conn.: Yale University Press, 1950), Chapter II. Others use a three-part scheme. Thus, Almond and Verba, following Parsons and Shils, discuss the cognitive, effective, and evaluative dimensions of political orientation. See Gabriel A. Almond and Sidney Verba, *The Civic Culture* (Princeton, N.J.: Princeton University Press, 1963), Chapter One.

plete until expanded to include a discussion of the distribution of political evaluations.

Now a new complication is introduced, for there is no simple relationship between mappings of information and mappings of evaluation. To illustrate, let us imagine the least complex of all situations. Consider one object of political relevance such as the Supreme Court. Suppose that the evaluative dimension of any individual's image of the Court were limited to the polar types "good" or "bad." Suppose furthermore that individuals could be classified dichotomously as having either much or little information about the Court. By crossing these two dimensions, we generate four types of images of the Court as schematized in the chart.

		Information about the Court	
		Much	Little
Evaluation	Good	I	II
of the Court	Bad	III	IV

In any random sample of American citizens we would surely find individuals representative of all four types. We would find those with little information evaluating the Court as both good and bad (types II and IV); and we would find those with much information also differing in their evaluations (types I and III). People are quite capable of having political opinions on subjects and issues about which they actually know little or nothing. Evaluations of all sorts are learned, and there is no rule of image formation which says that relevant information must be learned at the same time, or, for that matter, at any time.[6] A second point is that the interaction of information and evaluation is extremely complex. If we introduce a type IV person to more information about the Court, he may well reject the information entirely, thus remaining a type IV. On the other hand, he may accept some or all of the information and either

[6] For a discussion of opinion without information see Lane and Sears, *op. cit.,* Chapter Six.

change or not change his evaluation, thus moving toward type I or type III.[7]

Fascinating as the problem is, we cannot here enter into a serious discussion of the dynamics of individual image formation and change. Personality, group affiliations, age, religion, occupation, education, place of residence, use of leisure, and many other factors can contribute to the final equation. An extensive body of research and analysis examines the processes involved and the manner in which the operative variables change as the communicatory situation itself changes.[8] This is not, however, our prime concern, for it is not our purpose to characterize individual processes of change but rather to characterize entire political systems.

With this in mind, let us sum up and elaborate slightly the main points made so far in this chapter.

1. Data on channels and networks are incomplete without data on the distributions of politically relevant images which are the end products of communication. Although not stressed above, it is also important to relate distributions to networks. That is, when we characterize a system by saying that citizens A through M know thus-and-so about some object in the environment, it is probably also important to elaborate on the channels responsible for or supporting this image and its distribution.

2. Relevant images usually contain both information and

[7] An excellent introduction to the complexity masked here can be found in Philip E. Converse, "Information Flow and the Stability of Partisan Attitudes," *Public Opinion Quarterly*, Vol. XXVI, No. 4, Winter 1962, pp. 578-99.

[8] Although nominally devoted to literature relevant to the social psychology of the mass media, Wilbur Schramm, "Mass Communication," *Annual Review of Psychology*, Vol. 13, 1962, pp. 251-84, gives some feeling for the scope and content of publication in this area. Schramm's *selective* bibliography contains 232 references. See also Eleanor E. Maccoby, Theodore M. Newcomb, and Eugene L. Hartley, eds., *Readings in Social Psychology* (New York: Holt, Rinehart and Winston, Inc., 1958), Sections Two through Six. Extremely useful for the political scientist is Jack W. Brehm and Arthur R. Cohen, *Explorations in Cognitive Dissonance* (New York: John Wiley & Sons, Inc., 1962).

evaluation, and it is frequently difficult to separate the one from the other. Furthermore, it is common to find persons who hold similar evaluation images, at the same time holding different informational images. The converse is also true. Candidates for public office, among others, take cognizance of this fact. They and their supporters tend to use campaign communication to distribute an evaluational image: "X is the best man for the job." Except as it supports this image, candidates frequently behave as if they are not interested in the distribution of information, which of necessity is very uneven, imperfect, and open to evaluative ambiguity in any constituency. The end product sought by the candidate (acting as candidate rather than crusader) is the widest possible distribution of a positive evaluation of himself; the distribution of information is of secondary importance.

3. There are numerous ways in which we can map the distribution of politically relevant images in a society. Frequently we think of mappings onto sociodemographic attributes; we seek the distributions of informational and evaluational images by age, sex, occupation, income, education, place of residence, etc. There is a variety of other ways of dividing up the society. For instance, mappings can be made onto affiliations (Democrat, Republican), personality types (authoritarian, nonauthoritarian), personal experiences (fought in World War II, did not fight), political roles (bureaucrat, politician), or onto other images (for Red China in the UN, against Red China in the UN). In the abstract, the possibilities of classification are limitless, and the mappings themselves can run both horizontally and vertically through systems of social and political stratification. In the final analysis, as emphasized earlier, the configuration of images and other variables chosen depends on what aspects of system functioning the mapping is to illuminate.

THE FLOW OF IMAGES

In Chapter III it was argued that all political systems develop characteristic networks for handling communications of political consequence. In every system there is not one but many such networks, and the one or ones that are activated depend in part on the business with which the system is concerned at the time. Thus, in any country an agricultural problem calls into activity networks different from those set in motion by a foreign relations problem. Furthermore, an agricultural problem in the United States activates a type of communication subsystem different from an agricultural problem in the Soviet Union or India. The study of communication patterns can focus on both intra- and inter-system comparisons.

It was also argued that all systems to a greater or lesser degree exhibit structural elasticity. One aspect of this is that characteristic ways of communicating are sometimes modified or abandoned under the impact of unusual events (sometimes defined as events which the leadership chooses to *designate* as unusual). Within the limits set by the economy, geography, social structure, and political format, new patterns are then temporarily put in use. Precisely because these new patterns press against the limits imposed by the factors enumerated above, they throw the communication characteristics of a system into sharp relief.

An example from the American experience is illustrative. The assassination of President Kennedy affected habitual communication patterns in the United States in three primary ways.

1. *Speed and Diffusion of Information about the Event.* A national study made shortly after the assassination, found the following results:

> The President was shot at 12:30 P.M. (CST) on Friday; he was pronounced dead at 1 o'clock. By that time 68 percent, or two out of every three adult Americans, had heard the news. Within another hour, an additional 24 percent learned of the assassination, so that in less than two hours it appears that 92 percent of the public was aware of the event. By 6 P.M. the penetration had reached 99.8 percent. (Two of the 1,384 respondents told interviewers they did not hear of the assassination until the following day.) This abnormally fast and deep penetration of the news is probably without parallel in the past, although we have no comparable data concerning Pearl Harbor or the death of Roosevelt. Certainly, the fact that two-thirds of the public were reached in

one hour, 9 out of 10 in two hours, and almost everybody in less than four hours contrasts sharply with findings by Gallup and others that only rarely are more than 80 percent of the population *ever* aware of any given personality or event.[9]

2. *Channels and Networks Activated.* Under normal conditions in the United States, when a big news story "breaks," approximately nine out of every ten adults (of those who eventually learn) first find out about the event from the mass media. Subsequently, interpersonal channels come into play and the event is discussed and embedded in some framework of meaning.[10] In the case of the Kennedy assassination, however, only about one-half, 51 per cent, of the adult population received word through the mass media (overwhelmingly radio and television in this instance). The rest found out by telephone calls or personal messages.[11] The event so shocked and moved the population that adults told whoever was nearest at hand, friends, relatives, co-workers, or total strangers. This interpretation is supported by a study of a medium-sized California city where 46 per cent of the adults interviewed said that they first heard the news from some other person. Among this 46 per cent, as Table V.1 suggests, physical proximity was the overriding determinant of who informed whom.

3. *Levels of Intensity and Involvement.* As all studies of the assassination point out, the level of personal and institutional involvement generated by the events of the weekend was very high. Nothing else was to be seen on television, the normal recreational and business patterns of the nation were first disrupted and then suspended, and shock and grief spread through the population. The authors of the report on the na-

9 Paul B. Sheatsley and Jacob J. Feldman, "The Assassination of President Kennedy: A Preliminary Report on Public Reactions and Behavior," *Public Opinion Quarterly*, Vol. XXVIII, No. 2, Summer 1964, pp. 192-93.

10 See Bradley S. Greenberg, "Diffusion of News of the Kennedy Assassination," *Public Opinion Quarterly*, Vol. XXVIII, No. 2, Summer 1964, pp. 225-32, and the literature cited therein. See also the extremely illuminating studies and interpretations in Bradley S. Greenberg and Edwin B. Parker, eds., *The Kennedy Assassination and the American Public: Social Communication in Crisis* (Stanford, Calif.: Stanford University Press, 1965).

11 Sheatsley and Feldman, *op. cit.*, p. 193.

TABLE V.1 *Personal Source Informing Respondents Who First Heard about the Assassination from Others: by Location at Time of Being Informed*

	Location		
Personal source	*Home* (N = 60)	*Work* (N = 96)	*Away from home or work* (N = 36)
Spouse	12%	3%	3%
Other relative	35	2	6
Friend or neighbor	49	2	27
Co-workers	3	77	0
Stranger	1	16	64
Total	100%	100%	100%

Source: Greenberg, *op. cit.,* p. 229.

tional survey cited above characterize the atypicality of these patterns well:

> The Presidential assassination seems clearly to have engaged the "gut feelings" of virtually every American. Events of this order are extremely rare. Survey after survey has consistently shown that most people are normally preoccupied with their own health, their own families, their own problems, and those of their friends and neighbors. These are the things they talk about and worry about. A sizable proportion follow national and international events, many of them very closely, but their interest is largely that of a spectator watching a game. The election of an Eisenhower, the defeat of a Stevenson, a revolution in Cuba, the death of a Stalin — the surprise drop of an atomic bomb or the launching of a sputnik — such infrequent events, in contrast to the ordinary run-of-the-mill news, arouse the interest of almost everyone, but even they do not produce the cessation of ordinary activities, the almost complete preoccupation with the event, and the actual physical symptoms we have here described.[12]

The unusual speed and total diffusion of information, and the unusual patterns and networks activated — the two points

[12] *Ibid.,* p. 206. The physical symptoms referred to were such things as "had trouble getting to sleep," (48 per cent), "cried" (53 per cent), "felt very nervous and tense," (68 per cent).

previously made — are both causes and consequences of the high levels of intensity and involvement documented in the national survey. Only when an event strikes with such force do Americans stop strangers on the street to tell them about what has happened; and, on the other hand, only when an event of high and immediate drama dominates all mass media channels and many interpersonal ones as well do levels of personal involvement become so thoroughly reinforced and intensified on a national scale.

Unfortunately there are no similar data on events of like magnitude in either the United States or in other countries. Thus for comparative purposes, let us make up two examples. Suppose that in August 1961, Jânio Quadros, then President of Brazil, had been assassinated instead of resigning, as actually happened. Furthermore, in order to heighten the intensity of the event, suppose that the murderer was captured on the spot and turned out on investigation to be an agent of a foreign government. Here, then, are the essential ingredients of the most important political drama in the history of modern Brazil. How would communication about the event differ from the American case?

In the very top political and socioeconomic strata the news would travel rapidly, for these elites are plugged into the national system in much the same way as are their American counterparts. But soon informational attrition would set in. This is in sharp contradistinction to the American case, in which we noticed that intensity and personal involvement overrode normal rates and limits of diffusion and thus within hours almost 100 per cent of the adult population knew of the assassination. In Brazil, both the speed and total diffusion of information would be inexorably limited by lack of media facilities, by illiteracy, by geographical barriers, in short, by the entire panorama of nonpolitical communication constraints that have been reviewed previously.

In the absence of actual data, we cannot map this attrition, but some broad sociodemographic patterns can be imagined, based on what we already know about the diffusion of political information in Brazilian society. For instance, consider the following data on urban-rural differences presented by Lloyd Free in a study of a "national" sample of Brazilian adults.[13]

> It turned out that one-fifth of the urban and more than one-half of the rural samples could not name Kubitschek as the outgoing President of Brazil or Quadros as the newly elected President. (One illiterate in the rural sample said he wasn't sure who was President of Brazil but thought it was God.) Against this background it is perhaps not surprising that, when asked to identify the man who had served as President of the U.S. for the preceding eight years, 65% of the urban population and no less than 95% of the rural were unable to name Eisenhower — and even fewer, of course, could identify Kennedy as the newly elected President.[14]

Other data from this study suggest that the relationship between level of information and the urban-rural continuum in Brazil is quite direct. That is, when the urban population is stratified by size of city or town the pattern of attrition is also marked. When asked, "Who is the Prime Minister and top leader in Cuba?" the following distribution was found:

TABLE V.2 *Brazilians Able to Identify the Leader of the Cuban Revolution: by Place of Residence*

Place of residence: those living in	Identified Castro correctly
Cities over 500,000	50%
Cities from 50,000 to 500,000	42%
Towns from 2,000 to 50,000	26%
Rural areas	6%

Source: Free, *op. cit.,* p. 50.

[13] Lloyd A. Free, *Some International Implications of the Political Psychology of Brazilians* (Princeton, N.J.: Institute for International Social Research, September 1961). About his sample, Free says, "I have used the word 'national' in describing our cross-sections, but in the interest of accuracy must qualify that term: our samples, in fact, were almost but not quite nation-wide. To avoid nearly insuperable travel difficulties and unbearable expense . . . we excluded from our 'universe' about 9% of the national population living in the far northern . . . and central sections . . . which are large in area but very sparse in population" (p. v).

[14] *Ibid.,* p. 3.

We are confronted in the Brazilian case with the information consequences of the well-known syndrome of rural underdevelopment. It is compounded of poverty, ignorance, apathy, and isolation. Information about national events, no matter how momentous, simply cannot penetrate all these barriers in all cases. In the cities, however, geographical contiguity and other aspects of urbanization would support the eventual diffusion of information (possibly much distorted) to many sectors of the population not otherwise linked to the national scene through the mass media.

In both rural and urban environments it is doubtful that the networks activated in the diffusion of information about the assassination would differ greatly from those activated in the normal run of events. There is no great channel elasticity in such environments. Although diffusion would be a little more rapid and more complete than usual, nothing like the rapid 100 per cent coverage observed in the American situation could possibly occur.

As a final comparative exercise, imagine the assassination of Mao Tse-tung by a dissident petty official of the Chinese bureaucracy. How far and how fast would the information spread? Unlike the other two cases, the answers in this instance would depend primarily on how far and fast the authorities wished it to spread.

If, after some deliberation, it was decided to diffuse information about the event (with appropriate evaluative and contextual meanings attached) as widely and quickly as possible, an impressive apparatus of vertical communication could be activated. Newspapers and radio would distribute the "line" to as much as possible of the population at large and also to appropriate organizational nuclei. Then, through places of work, the party, the schools, study groups, the mass organizations, and all the rest of the familiar agitational channels the word would be passed on to the citizenry. Within a day or two, the coverage of the Chinese mainland would be amazingly complete. Although poverty, ignorance, apathy, and geographical isolation exist in China to a degree at least equal to the Brazilian case, most of their effect on the attrition of information would be obviated by the operation of these organizational networks.

The channel capacity and coverage of the Chinese system thus greatly exceed those of the Brazilian. But in one sense both systems exhibit limited elasticity, albeit of different types. In the Brazilian case, as noted above, limits are imposed on communication by economic, social, and geographical factors. In the Chinese case, the carefully planned and controlled organizational channels themselves define the upper limits of communication possibilities. These channels are in use *constantly* for a multitude of purposes, and thus what one observes are shifts in content and emphasis, not network contraction or expansion. This is another way of saying that the Chinese system operates at close to 100 per cent of its potential communication speed and capacity most of the time. There is little reserve for emergencies because by design the regime acts as if *most* vertical political communication were about matters of utmost urgency.

Enough has been said to give some feeling for the manner in which the American example and the hypothetical Brazilian and Chinese cases might be juxtaposed for comparison. A brief summary of some characteristics of information diffusion in the three systems following the assassinations, real and imagined, is contained in Table V.3.

Once again, as earlier in this chapter, the information component of image formation has received primary attention in our three examples. This was done in order to facilitate, under conditions of minimum conceptual complexity, the discussion of channels and patterns of diffusion. Yet, in each instance, the distribution of evaluations of the assassination is from the systemic point of view just as important as — if not more important than — the distribution of information about the assassination. In the American case, such matters were touched on in the brief section on levels of intensity and involvement. In the other two cases, since data were lacking, no attempt was made to hypothesize about evaluations. But it is clearly of great importance for comparative purposes to map patterns of evaluation onto the other variables that have been discussed. To use

TABLE V.3 *Diffusion of Information Following the Assassination of the Chief Executives of Three Nations*

	USA	Brazil	China
How does diffusion begin on a national scale?	Automatic, through the mass media	Automatic, through the mass media	Decision of political leadership
What channels are used for diffusion? [15]	Mass media, face-to-face (strangers), telephone	Mass media, face-to-face (strangers not too important)	Mass media, structured organizational channels
What channels predominate?	Mass media and face-to-face are equal	Face-to-face	Organizational channels
Are the patterns represented unusual?	Yes, mass media bypassed in favor of face-to-face	No (qualified), some media bypassing, but not much	No. Same patterns as usual.
What limits the rate of diffusion?	Fact that people are scattered at home, work, etc.	Impoverished economic and social environment	Nature of organizational channels. Need to control and explain.
What limits the scope of diffusion?	Almost nothing. 100% coverage possible	Social, economic, cultural factors	Extreme physical isolation, but coverage very high, eventually

the simplest of evaluative measures, think how much it would add to our examples if we could array the citizenry of each country along some continuum from "the assassination is a great evil" to "the assassination is a great good" and then present these data in aggregated form. If we could also gain some understanding of the more enduring perceptions of self,

[15] A distinction is made in this row between face-to-face channels and structured organizational channels (which frequently carry on communication in face-to-face situations). Face-to-face channels are the informal and unplanned linkages of relatives, friends, acquaintances, and even strangers. The phrase "structured organizational channels" retains the meaning given to it in Chapter III, where the planned and hierarchic aspects of communication in organizations were emphasized.

politics, and society which in turn condition evaluations of the events at hand, comparative analysis would be much enriched.

In closing, it should be emphasized that what has been attempted in the second half of this chapter represents only one of many possible focuses for the comparative study of the flow of images. We chose as an illustrative episode the assassination of the top political leader in each of three countries. The assassination, it was argued, triggers communication networks and results in patterns of informational and evaluational diffusion which are useful for both intra- and intersystem comparisons. On the one hand, we can see in what manner the diffusion is similar or dissimilar to what takes place when events of lesser magnitude are at the focus of attention. On the other hand, we can see the manner in which different types of systems handle events of at least nominal similarity.

In making this choice of examples, we have of necessity ignored other important types of flows. At least two areas of inquiry that have not been touched on deserve to be noted. First, we have paid little attention to lateral flows, either at elite or at lesser levels. Second, we have skipped over the entire topic of communication *up* political and social hierarchies. These omissions do not represent any devaluation of the importance of the two topics. In fact, both will enter into our discussion in the next chapter. In the interests of simplicity and brevity, only one set of examples was presented here. It is hoped that the framework in which these materials have been elaborated will also be of service in the study of other types of communication flow.

CHAPTER VI

Communication and the Performance of the Political System

IN THE last chapter we asked if it really makes any difference if nine out of ten adult Americans cannot name the members of the Supreme Court. We could ask hundreds of such questions about any political system. For instance, what difference might it make if nine out of ten Americans *despise* the Supreme Court? What if most Indians get no news about national politics? What if community development workers in Ghana habitually falsify reports to headquarters in order to cover up their shortcomings and advance themselves politically? What if one bureaucratic clique in Thailand hordes data on the economy in order to sabotage the operations of a rival clique? Examples, both real and imagined, could be multiplied endlessly, but all direct our attention to the same generic question: *Under what circumstances and to what degree is communication performance adequate for the functioning of a political system?*

This question, of course, cannot be answered in the abstract. Rather, it suggests a subject which in turn must be broken down before empirical analyses can proceed. This chapter is devoted to an exploration of the problem, but not to analyses of specific cases. As such, it is organized around the following four subheadings: (1) the adequacy of information; (2) the adequacy of motivation; (3) the adequacy of subsystems of communication; (4) the adequacy of links between subsystems.

Before continuing, it is necessary to say a few words about the concept of "adequacy" as it will enter the following discussion.

In any model of a political system which uses the language of functionalism, we are led to ask questions about structures. These could be the standard questions which enable us to relate structures to functions, which show, for example, that the communication activities associated with political socialization in China are carried on in the schools, the party, and the mass organizations. On the other hand, and most important for present purposes, these questions could be about the adequacy or inadequacy of communication performance for system functioning. That is, we can ask if the communication activities carried on in the schools, the party, and the mass organizations in China actually result in political socialization patterns that support the system.

However, because of its imprecision, the notion of "supporting the system" causes further difficulties. Communication activities may be more or less supportive of system functioning on at least three levels. At the lowest level, we can ask how fully communication activities support the execution and continuation of programs and policies of limited scope and duration. For example, were Chinese agitational efforts designed to enlist the energies of the population in the "kill-the-sparrows" campaigns adequate to the occasion? Did the people get out in sufficient numbers and actually kill birds? At the second level, we can ask how fully such communication activities aggregated in number and in time support the larger and more enduring organizational and policy goals set by the relevant leadership. Thus, we may want to know the net effectiveness of the Chinese mobilization and communication strategies in relation to the economic, social, and political tasks undertaken by the regime. This question is clearly more difficult to answer because the goals against which communication performance is supposed to be measured tend to be diffuse, internally inconsistent, and located in some unmapped future. Finally, we want to step completely outside of any evaluative framework tied to Chinese goals and ask about the *systemic* consequences of communication patterns and outcomes. At this most abstract level, we would want to know something about system stability, adaptability, development, and survival as they relate to communication patterns. Here arise most directly problems of short-term adequacy and long-term inadequacy. Are the tightly controlled exhortative structures which seem to serve current mobilization needs in China at the same time making difficult or impossible future adaptations, which will require flexibility and autonomy on the part of certain groups or persons? Are communication patterns and styles themselves flexible enough so that they can be adjusted as the environment in which the system operates changes and as new demands and dangers arise?

Any empirical analysis of the adequacy of communication performance for the functioning of a political system will probably touch all three levels. Certainly it is not possible, or at least not wise, to jump in at the third level and analyze system stability, adaptability, development, and survival without first grounding the analysis in the data generated by investigation at levels one and two. In the sections which follow, however, no attempt will be made always to keep separate the three levels masked by the notion of "supporting the system"; our only purpose here is to suggest some points of entry into the study of the relationship between communication performance and political functioning. As in other chapters, much simplication is necessary lest the discussion crumble under the weight of undue conceptualization.

THE ADEQUACY OF INFORMATION

At the beginning of an insightful chapter entitled "The Information Needs of a Complex Society," Kuhn presents the following parable:

> I need to know every color that passes beneath my window. So I have set up this machine, which will detect all the colors and make a record of them for me. But green makes me very angry, so I will smash the machine if it reports green. And tomorrow I may not like red, in which case I will smash it if it reports red.

But inaccurate information also makes me angry, so I will smash the machine if it reports wrongly, or if it fails to report.[1]

The author then points out that the functioning of any complex system, no matter how authoritarian its political format, requires that vast quantities of information flow through well-marked channels to designated audiences. Furthermore, the information that flows must be accurate if the system is to operate efficiently. Any autocrat acting in the willful manner described in the parable would sooner or later bring his house down around him. In fact, the historical record is littered with examples of rulers who have done just that. Moreover, even when considering the most open political formats, it is possible endlessly to multiply examples of policies and programs that have failed because of lack of information relevant to their design or execution. Political formats may be differentiated according to the manner and the extent to which flows of information are controlled and channeled, but all types of systems are subject to "information starvation" when choices and decisions must be made and the relevant data are not at hand.

There is, however, another side to the coin. Studies of the decision-making process frequently point out the consequences of information *overload*.[2] Too much information, arriving too fast and too "raw," can immobilize an individual or an organization. Consider the dilemma faced by an American deprived of his daily newspaper and given instead the entire 120,000 words of copy available in the main offices of the Associated Press.[3] Would his capacity to operate as either a citizen or a

[1] Alfred Kuhn, *The Study of Society* (Homewood, Ill.: The Dorsey Press, 1963), p. 771.

[2] The consequences of communication overload have been explored within the context of "crisis" and decision making under conditions of extreme time pressure. See, for instance, Charles F. Hermann, "Some Consequences of Crisis Which Limit the Viability of Organizations," *Administrative Science Quarterly*, Vol. 8, No. 1, June 1963, pp. 61-82, and the literature cited therein.

[3] See Wilbur Schramm, *Mass Media and National Development* (Stanford, Calif.: Stanford University Press, 1964), pp. 81-84, for a discussion of the causes of, and rate at which, information attrition occurs between the main office of a news agency and the local newspaper.

senator be in any way increased by the "completeness" of the information available to him?

The more general point is that in the first instance the adequacy of information in a system can be evaluated only according to the demands of system roles and role requirements. For instance, the role of American citizen probably does not require that one should be able to name the nine justices of the Supreme Court. This information is not relevant to satisfactory role performance. On the other hand, what if the individual in question, is not an ordinary citizen but rather a lawyer working in the Department of Justice? Then in order to operate successfully in his role he would need not only basic information about the structure and composition of the Court but also detailed information about its functioning. In the abstract, we can imagine drawing up specifications of the information requirements of innumerable roles in a political system. In reality, such specifications are very difficult to make because of the complexity of the role structure and because the boundaries of the information requirements shift according to the special demands of the moment. If we grant that the citizen need not know the names of the Justices of the Supreme Court, how far should his civic ignorance be allowed to extend before we consider him informationally unfit to participate in democratic politics? This, of course, is one of the classic problems of political theory, and one which continues to crop up with respect to the recently developing nations when critics ask how the populace, being poor, illiterate, politically inexperienced, and consequently uninformed, can possibly be expected to shoulder the full burdens of participant citizenship.[4]

---

[4] Other theoretical and normative dilemmas involve the interaction between information, role of performance, and political format. For instance, after a discussion of democracy in which he argues that the "rational" citizen will have only minimal political information because the costs of acquiring more information are very high and the returns are very low, Anthony Downs points out,

> government cannot force people to become well-informed for the following reasons:

Despite the impossibility of drawing up a complete set of information specifications for the various roles in a political system, it is still possible to make comparisons involving individuals and the information they possess. Here our interest frequently goes to rather extreme cases, defined as those instances in which information needed for role performance is either patently lacking or exceeded by some gross amount. Thus we have no trouble agreeing that the enfranchised citizen who cannot name any political party and the minister of agriculture faced with ten thousand pages of unaggregated and undigested statistics on crop acreages are both uninformed.[5]

A large area of indeterminacy still remains in which it is difficult if not impossible to make general statements about the adequacy of information for role performance, particularly as we move up the political hierarchy and as complexity increases. The information relevant to performance in any given role

---

1. There is no reliable, objective, inexpensive way to measure how well-informed a man is.
2. There is no agreed-upon rule for deciding how much information of what kinds each citizen should have.
3. The loss of freedom involved in forcing people to acquire information would probably far outweigh the benefits to be gained from a better-informed electorate.

In the face of these obstacles, most democratic governments do little more than compel young people in schools to take civics courses. — Anthony Downs, *An Economic Theory of Democracy* (New York: Harper & Row, Publishers, 1957), p. 247.

5 It is worth stressing that the notion of adequacy of information is quantitative only in the first instance. More important, as the parable opening this section reminds us, are the relevance and accuracy of information. As many have pointed out, even under totalitarian conditions, the systematic deception of an audience for political purposes has its limits as a strategy. Studies tracing the causes and consequences of misinformation, both planned and unplanned, in a political system frequently illuminate the system in telling fashion. See, for instance, the books which examine the classic "failure of intelligence" at the time of the Bay of Pigs invasion: Tad Szulc and Karl E. Meyer, *The Cuban Invasion: The Chronicle of a Disaster* (New York: Ballantine Books, 1962), and Haynes Johnson, *The Bay of Pigs* (New York: Dell Publishing Co., 1964).

changes as the environment of decision itself changes. In complex decisional units, what is adequate information at one point in time proves to be totally inadequate at another. In such circumstances, adequacy comes to refer to institutionalized ability to adapt to changing information requirements. We should focus then on the adequacy of the performance of specialized structures for information gathering and processing, not on the adequacy of the information itself.[6] The comparative study of the performance of these structures thus becomes, in some instances, the most viable approach to the subject.

THE ADEQUACY OF MOTIVATION

In the previous chapter a distinction was drawn between the informational component of an image and the evaluational component. This dichotomy is carried over into the present discussion as the distinction between the adequacy of *information* in a system and the adequacy of *motivation*. Kuhn establishes the basis of differentiation succinctly:

> Communication will thus be seen as having two possible major functions [purposes], the one to alter a receiver's concepts, which we will construe as the information function, the other to change his preferences or feelings, which we will construe as the motivation function. . . . To make the analysis as sharp as possible we will say that the first purpose is to inform, regardless of the effect on the receiver's preferences, and that the purpose of the second is to affect preferences without regard to the effect on information.[7]

[6] This subject is treated in more detail later in this chapter under the subheading *The Adequacy of Subsystems of Communication*. In the literature of organization theory the rational decision maker is in part defined as the individual who constructs his information-gathering apparatus so that it reports as quickly, accurately, and economically as possible on the relevant environment and changes therein. See Chester I. Barnard, *The Functions of the Executive* (Cambridge, Mass.: Harvard University Press, 1958), James G. March and Herbert A. Simon, *Organizations* (New York: John Wiley & Sons, Inc., 1958), and Herbert A. Simon, *Administrative Behavior* (New York: The Macmillan Company, 1958).

[7] Alfred Kuhn, *The Study of Society* (Homewood, Ill.: Dorsey Press, 1963), p. 181.

As emphasized in the discussion of images, any given communicatory act will probably be both informational and motivational in intent and effect.[8] Analytically, however, we profit by keeping the two aspects separate. Thus, just as in the previous section we suggested points of entry into the study of the adequacy of information for system functioning, so in this section we suggest analogous points of entry into the study of the adequacy of motivation.

A useful point of departure for the study of motivation and system functioning is the concept of legitimacy. Lipset defines legitimacy as follows, differentiating it from effectiveness:

> Effectiveness means actual performance, the extent to which the system satisfies the basic functions of government as most of the population and such powerful groups within it as big business or the armed forces see them. Legitimacy involves the capacity of the system to engender and maintain the belief that the existing political institutions are the most appropriate ones for the society. . . . While effectiveness is primarily instrumental, legitimacy is evaluative. Groups regard a political system as legitimate or illegitimate according to the way in which its values fit with theirs.[9]

[8] Informational and motivational communications are probably most frequently and most thoroughly mixed in revolutionary regimes. Consider the following problems taken from a mathematics wordbook used in Cuba in 1962 for adult education:

> There have been 3,000 lynchings in the United States in the last 20 years. What has been the average number of lynchings per year in that country?

> On August 6, 1945, a North American military airplane dropped an atomic bomb on the Japanese city of Hiroshima. The effects of this bomb were so awful that the population of 343,962 inhabitants was reduced to 137,197. How many inhabitants of Hiroshima did the atomic bomb dropped by the North Americans kill? How many years have passed since this barbarous act occurred? — Richard R. Fagen, *Cuba: The Political Content of Adult Education* (Stanford, Calif.: The Hoover Institution on War, Revolution, and Peace, 1964), pp. 68-69.

[9] Seymour Martin Lipset, *Political Man* (Garden City, New York: Doubleday & Co., 1960), p. 77. In the terminology used here, legitimacy is the result of certain patterns of motivation directed toward certain aspects of the political system, patterns which shift at different points in time and from

What does this actually mean? Certainly vocal minorities in the United States have strong negative evaluations of the Supreme Court and the manner in which it functions. Others reject as incompatible with democratic values the operations and even the existence of clandestine organizations such as the Central Intelligence Agency. How many institutions have to be rejected by how many people before the balance tips and we can talk of a failure of legitimacy in a system?

The question posed in this manner is unanswerable, but it does remind us of two other important areas of inquiry. First, as has been pointed out by Easton, there are at least three aspects of the political system for which some support (here defined as positive evaluations) must be generated.[10] There must be support for the political community, that is, support for the existing territorial arrangements, support for the regime or "rules of the game," and support for the government or those in power. Any person may withhold support at any one of the three levels, although individual patterns of nonsupport tend to be less inclusive as one moves from the community toward the government. That is, those who do not support the political community also tend not to support the regime or the government. Those who support the community but not the regime tend also to withhold support from the government, and so forth. There are also patterns of support and nonsupport within categories. For instance, an individual can have positive evaluations of some of the "rules of the game" (one man, one vote) yet have negative evaluations of others (Supreme Court justices appointed for life).

---

system to system. It should be clear that the study of systemic legitimacy does not exhaust the study of the adequacy of motivation. For instance, consider the Chinese kill-the-sparrows campaigns. Had the campaigns failed because of inability to change sufficiently the preferences or feelings of the masses toward sparrows, because of lack of free time, because of inability to kill birds, or for any other such reason, this would still not necessarily have signaled a failure of legitimacy. The system can survive the sparrows, and failure to motivate in this area does not threaten legitimacy, at least if such failures remain relatively infrequent and noncumulative.

[10] David Easton, "An Approach to the Analysis of Political Systems," *World Politics,* Vol. IX, No. 3, April 1957, pp. 383-400.

This takes us to our second area of inquiry. It makes a great deal of difference *who* as well as *how many* hold positive and negative evaluations of the different attributes of the system. To pick an extreme example, if 100,000 retail clerks feel that the Supreme Court is an inappropriate adjudicatory institution, this is not of the same order of systemic consequence as if 100,000 lawyers feel that way. The situation is similar in any hierarchy of roles or institutions that we care to map. Just as in the case of information, what can be considered a level of motivation adequate for system functioning depends on the roles we are considering, the objects for which support is being assessed, and the demands being put on the system at the time. In some instances, widespread apathy is adequate to ensure system functioning, in fact at times it is essential. In other cases, only the most intense and positive evaluative commitment will suffice.

In this and the previous section we have entered territory normally occupied at least in part by students of political socialization, and it would be well to detail the overlap before moving on. Our specific interest is in relating the performance of communication structures to the informational and motivational needs of the political system. We want to know if the recipients of political communication are informed and motivated in the ways that they must be in order to perform their roles and keep the system operating. Admittedly, we have difficulty in drawing up informational and motivational specifications for the different roles in any system. We have even more difficulty in determining where adequate performance in any role or sector shades off into inadequacy as measured against some norm of system survival, continuity, stability, or growth. Despite these problems, there is at least a single aim which informs the present enterprise: We wish to take stock of communication performance and somehow to judge it against criteria of system functioning.

The study of political socialization, on the other hand, begins with a different focus. Eventually, of course, the student of socialization wishes to know the consequences for political functioning of the processes, patterns, and content of political learning that exist in a system. In the first instance, however, the learning itself, not its consequences, is at the focus of inquiry. Of primary interest is the manner in which an individual acquires the skills — including information — motives, and attitudes necessary for coping with his political environment and participating (or not participating) therein. Thus, central to the study of political socialization is communication leading to change, growth, development, and adaption of individuals to a system. However, of little interest to the student of political socialization is communication activity which involves political actors but leaves them essentially unchanged as "political men," *even though the communication has important systemic consequences*. Our interests are different. Men are informed and motivated in important ways on many occasions when no socialization takes place. The men remain unchanged, but the system does not.

THE ADEQUACY OF SUBSYSTEMS OF COMMUNICATION

In the two previous sections the focus has been on individuals and on the adequacy of communication for the performance of the political roles that individuals hold. In this section there is a shift of emphasis. Now we concern ourselves with subsystems and ask if communication performance in the subsystem is adequate first for the functioning of the subsystem and second for the functioning of the larger political system. It should be clear that this shift of emphasis enables us to probe the subject matter from a different point of view, but it does not define a radically new set of concerns. Whereas first we might ask if the citizen or official is properly informed and motivated to discharge his responsibilities, we now ask if various structures perform in an adequate manner the communication tasks relevant to system functioning. These tasks might include informing and motivating all sorts of specialized audiences, building national consensus in critical areas of policy, or reporting salient information to members of the same or other systems. The crucial distinction is that in the first two sections the performance and relationships of agencies and channels of communication were not at the center of inquiry, and now they are.

An example may help to clarify this difference in approach and its consequences for the study of politics. If we ask questions about the adequacy of political information and motivation for role performance in a system, it is unlikely that our attention will be directed toward farmers as farmers because most role typologies of a political system would not include the relevant occupational breakdown. If, on the other hand, we ask questions about government agricultural policies, a new path of inquiry opens.

To limit the example, let us assume that our primary interest is in the implementation rather than in the formulation of agricultural policy. What are the communication questions that we might ask? Most obviously, there are at least three lines of inquiry. How do the farmers learn about agricultural policy, how do they acquire the information and motivation necessary for the implementation of policy, and how do the relevant governmental functionaries and decision makers learn about agrarian performance or nonperformance? The starkest outlines for a study of this communication subsystem are now in view. We have hypothesized initial communication from bureaucracy to clientele, subsequent communication of an instrumental nature intended to facilitate performance, and finally feedback from the clientele to the bureaucracy. Two comments are relevant: First, in evaluating the communication performance of this subsystem we must take into account the analytical and possibly the empirical independence of the hypothesized flows. For instance, adequate initial information in no way guarantees adequate informational and motivational communication in the instrumental stage although it may well facilitate such communication. Just because the farmers learn that cheap fertilizer is available does not mean that the government will succeed in convincing them that they should use it. Nor does success in teaching the farmers *how* to use fertilizer follow automatically from successfully convincing them that they *should* use it. Second, the agencies and channels used for the various types of communication may be quite disparate. Perhaps specialized mass media might carry the burden of disseminating information about policy aims, whereas, extension agents and other bureaucrats might be more important at the instrumental stage, and feedback on performance might come directly from the farmers themselves, from agricultural associations, or from officials specifically charged with reporting up the hierarchy.

Even in outline form, it is clear that we are dealing with a communication system of potentially great complexity. The number of points at which such a system can "fail" (in the sense of communication performance that is inadequate for the achievement of policy goals) is very large. Almost everyone is familiar with stories or studies which illustrate the breakdown of such systems: the farmers cannot be motivated to adopt new agricultural practices, or bureaucrats, fearing censure by their superiors, fail to report adequately on the performance or nonperformance of the clientele. Thus new communication efforts, based on false or incomplete information, go awry. It is not our purpose here to elaborate on the possible points of communication breakdown in subsystems; these would be as diverse as the systems themselves. Rather, the important effort involves bending this particular focus of inquiry to the service of comparative political studies.

How might this be done? There seem to be two strategies. First, it might be possible to index national systems according to the types of communication problems which chronically plague their subsystems. For example, some systems may be hindered by acute, culturally determined status differentials which render instrumental communication difficult. Recall that in Chapter IV the Thai bureaucracy was described as being essentially a one-way communication system, down the bureaucratic hierarchy to the public with no feedback. It is probable that other Thai subsystems are characterized by cultural patterns which inhibit feedback and interchange. Without making too many assumptions, we can imagine that the performance of the Thai system suffers at times from the consequences of what might be called "status communication." Officials at different levels of the hierarchy cannot talk to each other as frequently and openly as necessitated by the problems confronting the organization.

A second possible categorization of national systems might be based on the particular *policy* or *functional areas* in which subsystem communication is inadequate. This is a variant of the position that the operation of a political system is frequently best illuminated by an examination of the system's continuing problems or failures.[11] As political systems interact with changing national and international environments, their component subsystems are sometimes loaded in ways which prove too much for existing institutions. In Almond's words, the systems have not yet developed the capabilities necessary to handle incoming demands.[12] Among the most important capabilities that must be developed are those relating to political communication. The differentiated nature of the modern polity, however, makes it difficult to characterize an entire system as having inadequate communication. Problems have a way of testing subsystems, in foreign policy, agriculture, education, or welfare before challenging the system as a whole. On the other hand, the critical test may come in more diffuse fashion in some functional area such as political socialization or interest articulation. In either instance, the study of communication inadequacies in the relevant subsystem may well prove to be a telling point of entry into an understanding of the larger system.

THE ADEQUACY OF LINKS BETWEEN SUBSYSTEMS

In thinking about the adequacy of communication between subsystems in a polity, attention turns naturally to the notion of coordination and its bedfellow, control. The focus is natural because in most complex political systems considerable energy is of necessity devoted to ensuring, for instance, that the bureaucracy feeds to the legislature the policy-relevant informa-

[11] As an example of the utility of this type of analysis, see Roland Young and Henry Fosbrooke, *Smoke in the Hills* (Evanston, Ill.: Northwestern University Press, 1960). This is a study by a political scientist and an anthropologist of the failure of a government-sponsored agricultural terracing plan in Tanganyika.

[12] See Gabriel A. Almond and G. Bingham Powell, *Comparative Politics: A Developmental Approach* (Boston: Little, Brown and Company, forthcoming), Chapter II.

tion needed by the latter, that agency X cooperates with agency Y on joint task Z, or that some operative arm of government becomes linked to some social grouping in a manner which will facilitate desired political outcomes. Because of the tendency toward autonomy and self-aggrandizement in the subsystems of a polity, structural devices and proposals for structural reform proliferate whenever increased coordination and control at the national level are sought.

All political systems, then, can be characterized as having more or less adequate communication-coordination-control structures which link or fail to link semiautonomous subsystems.[13] This subject is central to both the theory and practice of democratic and nondemocratic politics. It is not particularly opaque, however, so we shall leave it at this point and concentrate for the remainder of this section on a related topic.

In Chapter IV we noted that communication patterns are affected significantly by the social and cultural diversities within a society, but this theme was not elaborated in detail at that time. Now we wish to develop it more thoroughly, paying special attention to the communication discontinuities which result from these diversities.

With the exercise of some license, we are shifting our focus from subsystems of the polity to subsystems of the society it-

---

[13] Hirschman gives an interesting example of the manner in which inadequate communication may affect the policy-making and policy-implementing processes in a developing society. He notes that

> If those who experience the result of mistakes are different from the policy-makers (i.e., the mistake-makers), correction depends on the latter being properly and rapidly informed by the former. If two-way communication between these two parties is poor, mistakes may have to be of large proportions to come to the notice of the policy-makers. Sharp policy changes may be justified on this ground until sufficient experience has been amassed or until better two-way communication between those who experience mistakes and those who make them has been established.

In the extreme case, communication between subsystems can be accomplished only if blunders are of such magnitude that ambiguity almost entirely disappears. See Albert O. Hirschman, *Journeys Toward Progress* (New York: The Twentieth Century Fund, Inc., 1963), p. 242.

self. The assumption is that communication discontinuities in the social system affect in important ways the conduct of politics. Nowhere is this more evident than in the less developed countries, and to them we turn for illustrative materials, bearing in mind that the more developed nations exhibit related discontinuities. The current politics of the United States and Canada are by no means free of problems deriving from basic cleavages in the racial and ethnic organization of the respective societies.

Let us consider the most extreme situation, the political schisms deriving from what Clifford Geertz has called "primordial sentiments" based on assumed blood ties, race, language, region, religion, and custom.[14] Geertz points out that in the new states subsystems organized around these bases of diversity have two important characteristics. First, they tend to have a high degree of internal cohesion, based precisely on the basic nature of the "tie that binds." They are also exclusive: one is born into the subsystem; one does not join. Second, the subsystem tends to be not a complement to, nor a component of, the larger civil society but rather to offer an alternative and competing definition of the political community. The problem is related to the discussion of legitimacy presented earlier in this chapter. That is, the intensity of primordial sentiments threatens the survival of the political system as loyalties based on class, party, or profession seldom do. In a telling passage, Geertz outlines the difference:

> Economic or class or intellectual disaffection threatens revolution, but disaffection based on race, language, or culture threatens partition, irredentism, or merger, a redrawing of the very limits of the state, a new definition of its domain. Civil discontent finds its natural outlet in the seizing, legally or illegally, of the state apparatus. Primordial discontent strives more deeply and is satisfied less easily. If severe enough, it wants not just Sukarno's or

---

[14] Clifford Geertz, "The Integrative Revolution: Primordial Sentiments and Civil Politics in the New States," in Clifford Geertz, ed., *Old Societies and New States* (New York: The Free Press of Glencoe, Inc., 1963), particularly pp. 111-13.

Nehru's or Moulay Hasan's head; it wants Indonesia's or India's or Morocco's.[15]

It follows that communication across the boundaries of these subsystems is difficult and confused. Lack of institutional links between the subsystems at times is a key factor. Additionally there is a lack of significant overlap between the political images held by members of one subsystem and members of any other. The phrase "they live in different worlds" captures the spirit of the discontinuity and its potential implications for the functioning of the political system.

Even if the schisms are not of the kind which threaten the bases of the political community, they continue to affect policy-making and policy-implementing processes if only because of the exclusivism and isolation which characterize the subsystems. Consider for a moment the problems of communication inherent in attempting to effect society-wide administrative action when there normally are few viable channels from the centers of political power to the periphery or between the subsystems to which members of the periphery in the first instance perceive themselves as belonging. A good example of such a situation and the resultant attempt to resolve it arose with the 1960 national census in Ghana. The administrative strategy called for a "head count" of all existing Ghanaians as of "Census Night," March 20, 1960.[16] Every dwelling in Ghana was to be visited during the following fortnight in order to secure a

[15] *Ibid.*, p. 111, punctuation added. The high point of *consensus* between subsystems seems to have been the preindependence period. Under colonial rule, not only were disparate territories and peoples forcibly held together, but also the various native elite factions were united in common action by the struggle against the imperial power. Once the imperial power is gone, once the struggle for independence is won, subsystem differences tend to reassert themselves. The patterns of thought and political rhetoric used to justify self-determination for the colony can easily be transferred to the justification of self-determination for the tribe, the ethnic group, the religious sect, or the subterritory. See Rupert Emerson, *From Empire to Nation* (Cambridge, Mass.: Harvard University Press, 1960), particularly pp. 119ff.

[16] The discussion of Census Night is derived from St. Clair Drake, "Traditional Authority and Social Action in Former British West Africa," *Human Organization*, Vol. 19, No. 3, Fall 1960, pp. 150-58.

list of all persons who had slept there on the twentieth. Two communication problems were critical. The people had to be informed of the impending census, and they also had to be motivated to cooperate in remembering and answering census questions when finally visited by an official. In order to alert the population to the significance of Census Night, a Census Education Committee was organized. For almost six months the Committee worked with films, leaflets, posters, radio talks, and mass meetings to direct public attention to March 20, called "A Night to Remember." Also the Committee worked through local chiefs. It was thought that the personal nature of census questions would arouse rural suspicions unless the prestige of the chieftancy could be associated with the effort. Moreover, it soon became obvious that without the aid of traditional authorities, it would not be possible to make the necessary precensus mapping of dwelling units. Just before Census Night, the regional Houses of Chiefs were urged to encourage full participation. One paramount chief even announced that "anyone who did not get himself counted would be banished from his state and would be numbered among the living dead!" [17]

In a communication environment such as the Ghanaian, despite the centralization of political authority, there are only a limited number of potential channels, either horizontal or vertical, which can be pressed into service for a national effort involving exchanges of information and motivation across subsystem boundaries. Moreover, as suggested earlier, the problem is not one which affects only the less well integrated systems. All polities from time to time experience the consequences of blocked and imperfect communication across subsystem boundaries. As the civil rights struggle in the United States attests, neither in the making nor in the execution of policy does there always arise between subsystems a dialogue of sufficient extent and coherence to sustain programs of national scope. Certainly the history of Western Europe also abounds in examples of separatism and primordial cleavages some of which remain

[17] *Ibid.*, p. 158.

crucial to an understanding of current political practices and problems.[18] These, however, are topics which lead us naturally into a discussion of political development, and that discussion must be held in abeyance until we have examined the relationship between political communication and political change.

[18] See Karl W. Deutsch, *Nationalism and Social Communication* (New York: John Wiley & Sons, Inc., 1953).

CHAPTER VII

Change in Politics and Communication:
Causes and Consequences

ON A NUMBER of occasions in previous chapters, potentially interesting and important topics have been bypassed with assurances that the subject would be treated in more detail in Chapter VII. Although it may have seemed so at the time, this was not simply a convenient device for ignoring or avoiding difficult topics. It was the result of a self-imposed ban intended to prevent the fragmentation of perhaps the key subject of the current study of comparative politics: *political change*. This rather lengthy chapter will be devoted to some ideas concerning the manner in which the study of communication can best be used to illuminate the political system in flux.

At first glance it would seem only proper to begin the discussion with some explication of what might be meant by the concept of political change. Instead, in line with our practice of attacking problems of definition in a formal manner only after alternative approaches have been exhausted, we shall begin with some descriptive materials which introduce possible relationships between communication, social change, and political functioning.

107

TWO MODELS OF COMMUNICATION AND CHANGE

Consider the following much compressed description of the mechanisms by which politically important ideas become diffused through a colonial system:

> Colonial powers often consolidate communication patterns in colonial areas which foster the spread of value-oriented beliefs such as nationalism. This consolidation is facilitated by establishing countrywide trading and communication patterns, imposing a common language, centralizing a colonial area politically, using mass media, and attempting to convert the population to a common religion.[1]

If we regroup and expand the ideas expressed here, we arrive at something like the following order of events leading to nationalism and colonial revolt: (1) Colonial powers, acting from both ideological and administrative motives, undertake certain practices which make possible more rapid and complete communication in the territories which they rule. The practices result in such changes as expanded media and transport facilities, growing physical and social mobility, urbanization, increased literacy, and language homogeneity. (2) As concomitants of these changes come important shifts in the content and distribution of political images. Individuals whose outlooks were once limited by tribal or regional self-identifications come to think of themselves as citizens of larger political communities. Leaders emerge who question the legitimacy of colonial rule; subsequently, they recruit followers and organize for political action. (3) Using the symbols, technology, and facilities first introduced by the colonial power itself, the nationalists move against their masters, and — if they are successful — independence ensues.

What do we find if we reduce to its most basic components the model of change which underlies this description? As we have suggested, there are three primary categories of events, linked as follows: (1) socio-economic changes with important

[1] Neil J. Smelser, *Theory of Collective Behavior* (New York: The Free Press of Glencoe, Inc., 1963), p. 337.

communication concomitants in channels, content, style, opportunities, etc., lead to (2) new ways of perceiving the self and the world which in turn lead to (3) behaviors which, when aggregated, are of consequence to the functioning of the political system.

It is clear that this is a model of great generality which both can be and has been used to describe sequences of events in a wide variety of circumstances. Although we chose to introduce the discussion with an example drawn from colonial experience, we could just as well have chosen an example from nineteenth-century England (increasing demands for participation and enfranchisement among the middle and lower classes) or from midtwentieth-century United States (civil rights and the Negro revolution). Perhaps the most general formulation of this view of communication and political change has been presented by Karl Deutsch.[2] His analysis is so important to our subject that it is worth outlining in some detail.

Deutsch begins his analysis with a definition of social mobilization "as the process in which major clusters of old social, economic and psychological commitments are eroded or broken and people become available for new patterns of socialization and behavior." [3] He then suggests typical constituent processes of social mobilization:

> . . . we may call m_1 the exposure to aspects of modern life through demonstrations of machinery, buildings, installations,

[2] See Karl W. Deutsch, "Social Mobilization and Political Development," *American Political Science Review,* Vol. LV, No. 3, September 1961, pp. 493-514.

[3] *Ibid.,* p. 494. The major clusters to which Deutsch refers are those signifying traditional congeries of economic and social relations. He focuses on the nation state as a unit of analysis, and thus his discussion derives from other more general discussions of the modernization process in national (traditional) societies. His formulation is equally useful, however, for the analysis of systems or subsystems in a nontraditional society. Thus, for example, it seems both legitimate and useful to think of the civil rights movement in the United States as deriving from the breakdown of "old social, economic and psychological commitments" in parts of the Negro (and white) communities even though the changes do not stem in the first instance from the "modernization" of a traditional system.

consumer goods, show windows, rumor, governmental, medical or military practices, as well as through mass media of communication. Then m_2 may stand for a narrower concept, exposure to these mass media alone. And m_3 may stand for change of residence; m_4 for urbanization; m_5 for change from agricultural occupations; m_6 for literacy; m_7 for per capita income; and so on.[4]

These constituent processes have two important characteristics. First, they tend historically to occur together. That is, where one finds increasing urbanization one is also likely to find change from agricultural occupations, increasing literacy, rising per capita income, and similar developments. Second, the processes tend to reinforce each other in a mutually supportive way. Literacy leads to increased gross national product per capita, which in turn leads to change from agricultural occupations, and so on in the familiar circular chain of cause and effect. Deutsch suggests that a prime task of theory is to take this causative system apart, study both its order and its deviance, and ultimately say with more precision just what types and patterns of social mobilization lead to just what political consequences. Lacking this detailed analysis, he nevertheless offers two propositions which relate social mobilization to the second and third elements of our model:

> In whatever country it occurs, social mobilization brings with it an expansion of the politically relevant strata of the population. These politically relevant strata are a broader group than the elite: they include all those persons who must be taken into account in politics. . . . The growth in the numbers of these people produces mounting pressures for the transformation of political practices and institutions. . . .
>
> Social mobilization also brings about a change in the quality of politics, by changing the range of human needs that impinge upon the political process. As people are uprooted from their physical and intellectual isolation in their immediate localities, . . . they experience drastic changes in their needs. They may now come to need provisions for housing and employment, for social security against illness and old age, for medical care. . . .

[4] *Ibid.*, p. 495.

They need, in short, a wide range and large amounts of new government services.[5]

The components of Deutsch's formulation are now in view, and they can be fitted into the three-part categorization previously used: (1) Social mobilization leads to (2) changes in what people know and how they perceive the world, which in turn lead to such developments as (3) expansion of the politically relevant strata of the population and changes in the quality and content of services demanded from government.

As emphasized previously, this model in its various guises informs much thinking and research on communication and political change. Such phrases as the "communication revolution" (referring primarily to developments in category one) and the "revolution of rising expectations" (referring primarily to developments in categories two and three) bear testimony to its pervasiveness in our current thinking. In our discussion we will designate it somewhat formally as the "model of exogenous change." The key point is that in analyses using this model, change is seen as a result of developments which occur *outside of* (independently of) the political system which in turn comes to be affected by the new patterns of communication. This is easy to see in Deutsch's formulation, where social mobilization, treated as a set of social and economic transformations, is the cause, rather than the consequence, of changes in the political system. Although less immediately obvious, it is equally true in our initial example in which the colonial power in the course of ruling stimulates the indigenous nationalism which subsequently transforms the internal politics of the colony, bringing it into open conflict with the mother country. The communication transformations which give rise to nationalism in colonial areas, in this view, are the byproducts of social, economic, and political developments of exterior origin.

As a final example, consider the instances of exogenous change which stem from technological innovation. These are often rather "pure" cases in which developments in the eco-

[5] *Ibid.*, pp. 497-98.

nomic sector come to influence the conduct of politics in important but unanticipated ways. For instance, the scientists, engineers, and businessmen who labored to perfect television probably gave little thought to the political implications of the new medium. Yet few would now deny that it has given a new cast and character and even a partially new set of rules to American politics.[6] It is equally clear that the impact has been essentially one way: in the United States television is changing politics, but the political system has shaped television only in the most marginal (regulatory) manner.

Variations on the exogenous model do not exhaust the conceptual vocabulary of those who concern themselves with changes in communication and the political system. There is another commonly used approach, which we shall here call the "model of endogenous change." In this the starting point is change *within* the political system itself. In its most compact form, this model also is reducible to three categories which can in turn handle a wide diversity of actual events: (1) Political strategies and forms of organization which directly or indirectly imply changes in communication patterns are selected. These

[6] The new cast, character, and rules which television brings (or is thought to bring) to politics are by no means always viewed with equanimity by political elites. For instance, note the following dispatch from South Africa:

The Government has moved to crush a new subversive movement here — the cult of the "little black box."

According to the Government this insidious movement has "destroyed mighty empires" and is now seeking nothing less than "the destruction of white South Africa."

The cult consists of those who seek to bring television to South Africa. Its leaders are alleged to be Harry F. Oppenheimer, chairman of the powerful Anglo-American Corporation, and other "mining interests.". . .

Now, Dr. Albert Hertzog, the Minister of Posts and Telegraphs, has declared open war on the cult. In a statement to the Government paper *Die Vaderland,* Dr. Hertzog said:

"The overseas money power has used television as such a deadly weapon to undermine the morale of the white man and even to destroy great empires within 15 years that Mr. Oppenheimer and his friends will do anything to use it here.". . . — *The New York Times,* November 10, 1964, p. 1.

patterns, once in operation, lead to (2) new ways of perceiving the self, the world, and politics (including new definitions of proper and improper political behavior) which in turn contribute to (3) changes in the functioning of the political system (although perhaps not the changes anticipated by those who implemented the new strategies and forms of organization). As can be seen, the exogenous and endogenous models differ most markedly in category one, the locus of the primary stimulus to change in communication patterns. Additionally, however, there is a purposefulness or directedness about the endogenous case which is lacking in the exogenous model. In the endogenous case we are speaking about situations in which leaders set out to rectify "conditions" through either the creation of new political resources or the exploitation in an innovative manner of existing resources. Communication changes are both the instrument and the consequence of this policy-oriented leadership. Whether or not in the final analysis the desired systemic changes actually occur, whether the citizens actually become more participant, the bureaucracy more responsible, or the farmers more knowledgeable is another question. But the initial push comes from the political sector, and the related communication developments, if not ultimately confined to that sector, are at least originally manifested there.

Perhaps some examples of endogenous change will help to clarify the discussion. In the previous chapter we mentioned instances of governmental information and motivation campaigns, and such efforts qualify as endogenous under our definition when in fact new communication facilities (e.g., an agricultural extension service) are created in order to make possible the implementation of new policies. At times such changes are truly massive in the sense that the new policy objectives of the leadership call for nothing less than the transformation of existing patterns of political communication and the creation of a new set of structures, relationships, and linkages. A case in point is Cuba after the Castro takeover in 1959. A simple checklist of communication-relevant changes made during the first four years under Castro serves to give some feeling for the pervasiveness of the transformation.

The substantial mass media system was taken over by the government and used for spreading the revolutionary gospel. "Counterrevolutionary" voices were silenced. An impressive array of specialized publications blossomed.

The pre-Castro army and navy were destroyed; the Revolutionary Armed Forces (with compulsory military service since late in 1963) and the militia were organized to take their place. In addition to defense, these organizations have important political education functions.

A host of mass organizations — for workers, women, youth, students, and farmers — was formed. Cast in the Leninist tradition, these have become key "transmission belts" linking the leadership to the citizens. They also have important educational functions.

The school system was completely transformed. A massive adult literacy campaign was launched in 1961 and training in both skills and politics continues in a variety of types of adult schools. In addition, "Schools for Revolutionary Instruction," having as their fundamental task, "the ideological training of revolutionaries and, in turn, of the people," [7] have been established throughout the island.

As an overall instrument of coordination and control, a new Marxist-Leninist party is being constructed. When recruiting is complete and the party fully operative, it should (so the leadership hopes) give new unity and coherence to the activities of the other agencies of political communication and socialization sketched above.

As can be appreciated from even this cursory checklist, we rightly call such changes revolutionary.

There are other types of transformations, less massive, which also fit the endogenous model and illustrate the communication consequences of political reorganization. Consider the authoritarian stabilizations which have been endemic in the developing nations since the end of World War II. By authoritarian stabilizations we mean the actions of elites who suspend or ignore the particular range of procedures and struc-

[7] Fidel Castro, as quoted by Lionel Soto in "Las Escuelas de Instrucción Revolucionaria en una nueva fase," *Cuba Socialista* (Havana), Año IV, No. 30, Feb. 1964, pp. 62-77. Quotation on p. 63.

tures (elections, civil rights, etc.) usually associated with the Western model of democracy. These may be military or non-military elites and they may come to power by "constitutional" or "unconstitutional" means.

Elites explain and excuse these stabilizations by using two types of arguments. The first we can call the "tutelary" argument. Here it is claimed that the citizens (and often the politicians themselves) are "not ready for" the institutions provided in the constitution. Members of this school of thought often regard the unlettered masses as "political children" and (other) politicians as greedy, corrupt, and self-seeking. The second explanatory argument concentrates on the inadequacy of institutions rather than on the inadequacy of men. This can be called the "emergency" argument. Proponents of this school say that the developmental tasks facing the new or developing states are too monumental to be met successfully under pluralistic political arrangements.[8] As can be seen, these arguments are related.

Under authoritarian stabilizations there may be several types of change in patterns of communication. The tutelary argument suggests that communication *up* the political hierarchy can be sharply curtailed, since the elites already "know better" than the citizens what the latter want and need. Thus, there is no need to consult the people — through elections or other structures — since the preferences of the common man do not constitute significant inputs into the political process under this scheme.

On the other hand, the emergency argument suggests among other things that communication *down* the hierarchy must be

[8] The rhetoric of politics and the language of analysis come strikingly close together at this point. Many scholars, seeking explanations for the pervasiveness of authoritarian reorganizations, fasten on the same arguments and use much the same terminology as do the indigenous elites. For instance, ". . . the capacity for action of parliamentary governments is apt to prove inadequate to the heroic demands of rapid development," Robert L. Heilbroner, *The Future as History* (New York: Harper & Row, Publishers, 1960), p. 85. For statements by indigenous elites, see Paul E. Sigmund, Jr., ed., *The Ideologies of the Developing Nations* (New York: Frederick A. Praeger, Inc., 1963). The discussion presented here owes much to Edward Shils, *Political Development in the New States* (The Hague: Mouton, 1962).

substantially increased, since "enlisting the aid of the masses" is fundamental to all ambitious developmental plans. Even the special variation on the emergency theme used in the United States during World War II involved increased downward communication in the form of exhortative campaigns intended to encourage the citizenry to do such things as buy bonds, save tin cans, enlist in the armed forces, and send packages to servicemen.

Although this is an obvious simplification of an immensely complex set of relationships, the following generalization seems defensible. Authoritarian stabilizations do not simply imply increased insulation of elites from citizens. Rather, they suggest that a decrease in certain types of communication up the hierarchy is coupled with an increase in total communication down the hierarchy. Although elections may be suspended and critics of the ruling elite may be silenced, feedback from the masses in some form remains necessary if official action programs are to be related to social reality.

We have been concentrating on the elite-mass ramifications of authoritarian stabilizations, but the elite-elite relationships are perhaps of equal importance. Elites that are "out" are condemned to silence. "Disruptive criticism" cannot be tolerated by the incumbent leadership, and therefore controls over many channels of communication are tightened. Not only is control necessary for negative reasons (to prevent incitement and criticism), but control is necessary also for positive reasons (to gain access to channels in order to promulgate new ideas, dicta, and images of politics). The most immediate targets of increased control may well be the mass media, but subsequently controls might be extended to cover such channels as the trade unions and student organizations. In such circumstances the Western concept of "the loyal opposition" is interpreted as self-contradictory. As one African leader has said, "This [national development] calls for the maximum united effort by the whole country if it is to succeed. *There can be no room for difference or division.*" [9]

[9] Julius Nyerere, "One-Party Rule," *Atlas*, March 1962, p. 186. Emphasis in original.

The discussion of endogenous change in Cuba and in instances of authoritarian stabilization has left almost untouched categories two and three of the model. That is, we have not explored linkages between communication change, changes in perceptions, behavior, and ultimately the consequences for the functioning of the political system. To do so in the abstract and in the absence of reliable data is difficult for two reasons. In the first place, the chain of events triggered by the massive endogenous changes in Cuba has not by any means run its course. Strategies have been articulated and put into practice, but the effects of these strategies, on individuals, subsystems, and the national system, are incomplete and difficult to evaluate. At the moment, the most telling way to characterize the Cuban system is to describe the new forms of organization that have been instituted and the new goals that have been expounded. We can characterize the consequences of these transformations for the patterning and control of political communication, but we cannot, as yet, make a satisfactory analysis of the long-range effects or adequacy of the new patterns. In short, the type of analysis suggested in the previous chapter, in which communication performance is related to political functioning at a number of levels, is not yet possible in Cuba.

In the second place, and now we turn to the authoritarian stabilizations where the point is better illustrated, the consequences of politically triggered communication changes depend on many factors other than the nature of the strategies adopted. This was also hinted at in the previous chapter when we mentioned that the unanticipated consequences (including failures) of communication programs frequently loom as large, and are as interesting, as the expected consequences. Communication changes accompanying authoritarian stabilizations — increased control over the mass media, the silencing of elite dissent, burgeoning motivational and informational campaigns directed toward the masses — may contribute to any number of types of political transformations. Just what form these transformations will take, if they occur at all, is not immediately obvious from any reading of the strategies themselves, for many different forces work to block, attenuate, and redirect the strategies that the elites inaugurate.

BRINGING THE MODELS TOGETHER

Until now, we have been talking about the exogenous and endogenous models as if they were somehow exclusive ways of describing change. They are not, of course, and the time has come to rectify the distortions introduced by the particular order of presentation followed in this chapter. That exogenous and endogenous communication change become intertwined in ongoing political systems should come as no surprise. The economic, sociocultural, political, and historical factors introduced in Chapter IV as determinants of communication patterns are always operative in communication change (albeit in more or less muted form) if only to establish limits beyond which change cannot occur. We have singled out the instances in which *politics* is the prime mover and here named them collectively the endogenous case, holding them up for comparison against all other instances which we call collectively the exogenous case. What has been gained by this, and how can we both resolve and justify the distinction we have drawn? Because there are more data available and because key relationships are easier to characterize, let us investigate these questions through a brief analysis of mass media growth and political change.

As a starting point, recall Tables 1 and 2 in Chapter IV. There it was shown that nations economically well developed and having high rates of literacy tend also to be rich in mass media facilities. The obverse, of course, is also true. These tables could be expanded to relate other variables indexing modernity (urbanization, per capita energy consumed, proportion of children in primary school) to levels of mass media development. When this is done, consistently strong relationships between the modernity variables and the mass media variables are found.[10] What this shows is that historically mass

[10] For instance, consider the correlations between radio receivers per 1000 population and the following variables (product moment correlation coefficient in parentheses): urbanization (.66); motor vehicles

media growth has been a concomitant of economic and social development. Although the correlations themselves tell us nothing about causality, it is clear that the mass media have been both cause and effect, both mover and moved, in the complex interplay of factors which we call the modernization process. There have been some notable attempts to analyze this process, separating out the role of the mass media and other variables in order to make more precise statements about the order of change and the parts played by various elements at various stages of modernization.[11] For our purposes, we can treat the entire complex as exogenous change, change which originates outside of the political system and issues in transformations which ultimately affect the conduct of politics.

There is another side to the coin. Not only do the mass media grow as systemic elements and concomitants of the modernization process, they also grow because political elites, at least in some countries, decree that they should. This, of course, is endogenous media development and it becomes overlaid and mixed with the exogenous development discussed above. The rate and scope of endogenous development depend both on the characteristics of the regime and on the technology of the media. The political format most congenial to directed media growth is the Leninist, where government ownership, control, and exploitation of mass communication are integral parts of the ideology of social and political change.[12] However,

---

per 1000 population (.83); steel consumed per 1000 population (.87); energy consumed per person (.80); calories per day per person (.60); proportion of children 5-14 in primary school (.73). Data from Wilbur Schramm and W. Lee Ruggels, "How Mass Media Systems Grow," in Daniel Lerner and Wilbur Schramm, eds., *Communication and Change in the Developing Countries* (Honolulu: East-West Center Press, forthcoming).

[11] The most influential attempt to analyze the modernization process with special reference to the mass media is Daniel Lerner, "Communication Systems and Social Systems. A Statistical Exploration in History and Policy," *Behavioral Science*, Vol. II, No. 4, October 1957, pp. 266-75. See also Daniel Lerner, *The Passing of Traditional Society* (Glencoe, Illinois: The Free Press, 1958), particularly Chapter Two. The most cogent critique and modification of Lerner's argument is Schramm and Ruggels, *op. cit.*

[12] See Ithiel de Sola Pool, "The Mass Media and Politics in the Modern-

even in less total formats such as the mobilization systems mentioned in Chapter IV, elites articulate developmental ideologies which incorporate ambitious plans for expanded media facilities designed to be used in the service of the state. Particularly attractive in media-oriented developmental schemes are the electronic media, independent as they are of the constraints imposed by geographical isolation and illiteracy. But the special advantages of print are also recognized by many planners, and one often finds politically stimulated growth in the electronic media coupled with ambitious long-range plans for increased literacy and expansion of newspapers and periodicals.

Endogenous media growth has not continued long enough in enough countries to affect greatly the aggregate statistics presented in Chapter IV and elaborated above in the discussion of exogenous change. That is, the best predictors of a country's level of media development, no matter what its political format, are still such variables as its level of literacy, per capita gross national product, and per capita consumption of energy. When we turn to *rates* of media growth, however, rather than to absolute *levels,* the picture changes. Here we can detect the incipient effects of planned endogenous media expansion, for countries identifiable either as Communist or as modernizing under mobilization formats are growing demonstrably faster in certain media than are other nations.[13] Moreover, and this is perhaps most important, media capacity is being increased not as the concomitant of socioeconomic development, but rather self-consciously as an instrument of change and rule, forged by, and remaining in the hands of, the politi-

---

ization Process," in Lucian W. Pye, ed., *Communications and Political Development* (Princeton, N.J.: Princeton University Press, 1963), and Ithiel de Sola Pool, "The Role of Communication in the Process of Modernization and Technological Change," in Bert F. Hoselitz and Wilbert E. Moore, eds., *Industrialization and Society* (Paris: UNESCO, 1963).

[13] This point is elaborated and supported in two related articles: Richard R. Fagen, "Relation of Communication Growth to National Political Systems in the Less Developed Countries," *Journalism Quarterly,* Vol. 41, No. 1, Winter 1964, pp. 87-94; and Richard R. Fagen, "Mass Media Growth: A Comparison of Communist and Other Countries," *Journalism Quarterly,* Vol. 41, No. 4, Autumn 1964, pp. 563-67, 572.

cal elite. In the modern world it is thus technologically possible — and to some it looms as politically desirable — to deviate on occasion from the historical patterns and constraints which have characterized media growth over the past several centuries. The juxtaposition of television and the oxcart in parts of Asia, Africa, and Latin America bears witness to these possibilities.

It is difficult to predict the political consequences stemming from the introduction of the mass media into societies which are not "ready" for them in the historic-economic sense. At the very least, however, the possibility of so introducing them has led to some rethinking among elites concerning what constitutes a viable policy of political communication in the modern world. The following statement by Nasser is illuminating:

> It is true that most of our people are still illiterate. But politically that counts for far less than it did 20 years ago.
> Literacy and intelligence are not the same thing. Radio has changed everything. Once the villagers had no knowledge of what was happening in the capital. Government was run by small coteries of people who did not need to take account of the reactions of the people, who never saw a newspaper or could not read it if they did.
> Today people in the most remote villages hear of what is happening everywhere and form their opinions. Leaders cannot govern as they once did. We live in a new world.[14]

Furthermore, as Lerner and others have pointed out, there is a range of consequences, potentially of great import, which derives in part from the interaction between the rapid growth of the mass media and the postcolonial explosion in political participation.[15] The expansion of popular suffrage and other forms of mass involvement in politics since the end of World War II has not necessarily been accompanied by a parallel expansion (as happened in much of Europe and the United States) of literacy, economic well-being, social mobility, or political capability. Millions of persons who two decades ago would not have been aware of, much less participant in, na-

[14] Quoted in Lerner, "Communication Systems and Social Systems," p. 274.
[15] *Ibid.*, pp. 273-74.

tional politics now have access to a radio and a vote on the one
hand and political organizations and symbols on the other.
They have acquired political rights and expectations and in
turn articulate demands which challenge existing policies and
practices. The media, at least in traditionally media poor set-
tings, accelerate the pace at which these demands are formulated
and articulated while contributing little to an environment
conducive to their satisfaction.[16]

We have now come full circle in our argument. The hypothesized political consequences of media growth — in this case
increased demands for participation and services — are the
same as those noted by Deutsch in his more general discussion
of the consequences of social mobilization. This comes as no
surprise because Deutsch specifically mentions mass media
growth as one of the "constituent processes" of the mobilization syndrome. What is being emphasized here, however, is
that even when concerned with social mobilization (first introduced as an example of exogenous change) we need not
confine ourselves to a view of political change in which the communication transformations of relevance occur wholly outside
of the political system. On the contrary, social mobilization can
be treated equally well within the endogenous model if we can

---

[16] This argument, of course, need not be confined solely to the mass
media or in the first instance to politics. Time and again in the literature
dealing with communication and social change we encounter variations on
the theme that Lerner has called "The Revolution of Rising Frustrations."
[See Daniel Lerner, "Toward a Communication Theory of Modernization.
A Set of Considerations," in Pye, ed., *op. cit.*] The basic idea is that social
mobilization and its psychic concomitants tend to outrun the system's
capacity to create new roles and new opportunities for participation in the
society, the polity, and the economy. Individual aspirations and expectations outstrip the system's assimilative capacity; or, in Lerner's telling language, the ratio of "wants" to "gets" increases at an unprecedented rate
under the impact of twentieth-century communication technology. Necessarily, the revolution of rising frustrations has political implications even
if in the first instance the wants are not directed toward objects usually
thought of as political. Thus, demands for new types of participation in
the economy (as producers, consumers, etc.,) rather quickly assume political
importance in situations where the economic environment offers only a
limited panorama of new roles.

succeed in showing that the constituent processes stem from indigenous political policies and practices. In fact, the relevance of the endogenous model is bound to increase because of the amount of political experimentation occurring in the modern world and because of the impressive array of communication technologies, both material and social, available to the experimenters. On the other hand, as the discussion of mass media growth was intended to indicate, a full understanding of the relationship between communication change and political change cannot depend exclusively on either model, for both contribute to our understanding in most instances.

COMMUNICATION AND POLITICAL DEVELOPMENT

In the preceding sections, we have concentrated on the relationship between communication change and political change. Although no formal definition of political change has been offered, the examples chosen suggest that we were referring to what Almond and Powell call "systemic change," changes which affect in some basic manner the functioning of the national political system and result in structural, cultural, and performance patterns palpably different from those operating earlier.[17] Changes characterized in this manner have no necessary "direction." By this is meant that we cannot isolate any single dimension or set of dimensions and say that systemic change necessarily involves movement from less to more (or from more to less) of the attributes or characteristics in question. To pick some very gross categories, let us consider

[17] See Gabriel A. Almond and G. Bingham Powell, *Comparative Politics: A Developmental Approach* (Boston: Little, Brown and Company, forthcoming), Chapter II. As examples of two types of change, the first not systemic and the second systemic, Almond and Powell discuss Britain and Ghana during the past decade. In Britain, they note, despite new leadership and changing international and domestic policies, the system as before is still open, responsive, and dependent on a highly specialized set of structures which continue to perform in much the same fashion as they did ten years ago. In Ghana, on the other hand, a rather massive authoritarian stabilization has issued in new patterns of decision making and response, and a new set of rules governing the relations between the incumbent elites and potential or actual counter-elites.

political change in Germany over the last six decades — from Empire to Weimar to National Socialism to the postwar division and subsequent developments. These political transformations have involved changes in interelite relationships, structural arrangements, civil liberties, mass participation, and system performance which, although massive, are certainly not unidirectional.

On the other hand, when our attention turns to political *development,* the very phrase itself suggests that we are dealing with a class of transformations having certain directionalities in common.[18] What might these be? In other contexts in which the word "development" is used, even the nonspecialist often receives a rather clear and immediate picture of what in fact is changing when the organism or system is said to be developing. Thus, as a first approach to the meaning of *child* development we visualize change from more to less reliance on parents, from lesser to greater levels of linguistic and physical skill, and from less to greater ability to defer immediate gratifications and rewards. Similarly, with the notion of *economic* development we associate such things as change from lesser to higher levels of per capita income, movement away from barter relationships toward the use of money, and an increased capacity to use technology in the service of production and distribution. It is indicative of the shorter history of the concept of political development and perhaps of the particular intractability of the subject that in popular usage there is no immediate and common interpretation of just what is changing when political development takes place.

There are, however, a number of convergences in current writing about political development, and one formulation in particular is so intimately tied to a communication approach to the study of politics that it deserves special emphasis. At some risk of imposing more order on the field than actually exists, we can say that there is emerging a school of thought in which *political development is viewed primarily as a process of national integration, as movement from less to more na-*

---

[18] In the discussion of political development we are also, of course, still dealing with systemic political change. However, now we specify and treat only a subtype of the genre.

tional unity. If left without elaboration, this formulation obscures as much as it reveals about the actual content of this point of view. Thus for the next few pages we shall turn our attention to an explication of what is usually meant when political development is treated as movement toward greater national unity.

As a beginning, consider a vivid passage written over a century ago in which Karl Marx described the French peasantry as follows:

> The small-holding peasants form a vast mass, the members of which live in similar conditions but without entering into manifold relations with one another. Their mode of production isolates them from one another instead of bringing them into mutual intercourse. The isolation is increased by France's bad means of communication and by the poverty of the peasants. Their field of production, the small holding, admits of no division of labour in its cultivation, no application of science, and therefore, no diversity of development, no variety of talent, no wealth of social relationships. Each individual peasant family is almost self-sufficient; it itself directly produces the major part of its consumption and thus acquires its means of life more through exchange with nature than in intercourse with society. A small holding, a peasant and his family; alongside them another small holding, another peasant and another family. A few score of these make up a village, and a few score of villages make up a Department. In this way, the great mass of the French nation is formed by simple addition of homologous magnitudes, much as potatoes in a sack form a sack of potatoes.[19]

With few changes, Marx's characterization of France and his metaphor of the "sack of potatoes" could be used to describe the sociopolitical attributes of the countryside in any of the less developed systems which now occupy our interest. Political development, in this instance, would involve linking together the individuals, families, and local decisional units which coexist but do not interact in the peasant society.

[19] Karl Marx, "The Eighteenth Brumaire of Louis Bonaparte," in *Karl Marx and Frederick Engels: Selected Works in Two Volumes*, Vol. I (Moscow: Foreign Languages Publishing House, 1962), p. 334. The "Eighteenth Brumaire" was written and first published in 1852.

Related to this first point is a second that is even more frequently mentioned in the literature which defines political development as movement toward national unity. Almost all authors who address themselves to this theme refer to the discontinuities which separate elites in the less developed system from the masses that they purport to rule. The problem was touched on in the final section of the previous chapter, but it is more complex than the discussion at that time indicated. In the broadest sense, the discontinuities are cultural. For instance, in Africa and Asia colonization diffused Western languages, education, customs, ideologies, and organizational forms very unevenly through the social system. Most of the population was hardly touched. In other areas the interplay of exogenous and endogenous change has also produced a most uneven distribution of the physical, behavioral, and cognitive aspects of "modernity." It is not difficult to imagine that a French-educated Peruvian intellectual would feel more "at home" in the company of his Parisian counterpart than with an Indian from the Andean altiplano. Supposing no language barrier, what would the intellectual and the Indian talk about? In ordinary parlance, what do they have "in common"? The furnishing of these two minds would be greatly dissimilar; their images of past, present, and future would hardly overlap.

The political concomitants of these cultural discontinuities are familiar: the fragmentation of the political process, the prevalence of cliques, the emergence of charismatic leadership, and so forth.[20] Even when some tentative organizational bridges are built across the chasm, the basic problem of finding common cultural ground persists. Marriott gives an interesting example from his experience in India.

Consider a typical debate between one rural development officer and a conservative Brahman farmer, a key man in his village. The officer's aim was to persuade the farmer to adopt the practice of sowing, then plowing under, a green crop in order to enrich

[20] In this listing is implied the model of "transitional politics" as developed by Lucian Pye and others. See Lucian Pye, *Politics, Personality, and Nation Building* (New Haven, Conn.: Yale University Press, 1962), Chapter Two.

the soil for subsequent planting of grain. The development officer's initial secular appeals to economic advantage had gone unheeded, and had in fact been exposed as not only self-seeking but also sinful, since plowing a crop under involved taking the life of the destroyed plants. The officer next appealed to the doctrine of duty as set forth in the sacred Gita. Here his words went over the heads of most villagers, while failing to equal the much greater traditional textual learning of his Brahman antagonist. Success came to the officer only when he put himself into the nonliterate peasants' own dilemma and spoke of the need for reconciling the inevitable sins of farming with the possibility of earning greater spiritual merit by applying the farmer's wealth to the performance of social and religious duty.[21]

The discontinuities which separate the elites from the masses in the less developed system are manifold and mutually reinforcing, and the more strictly political aspects of national integration cannot be understood without some prior understanding of the geographic, cultural, and economic matrix which shapes political behavior and the political dialogue.

In summary, then, two problems engage the attention of those who view political development as the movement from less to more national unity. The first is the sack-of-potatoes problem, the necessity of linking previously autonomous (but similar) units with each other. The segmented society must be transformed into a national society with all of the interdependence, division of labor, and specialization that the latter implies. The second is what might be called the "homogenization" problem, the necessity of creating institutions and a political style which can bridge the gulf between the national elites and all the others who at least nominally are members of the same polity. A common frame of political reference and action, national in scope, must be found.

We have already suggested why the national integration approach to political development finds its natural ally in the study of communication. No one has seen this more clearly or argued the point more forcefully than Lucian Pye.

[21] McKim Marriott, "Cultural Policy in the New States," in Clifford Geertz, ed., *Old Societies and New States* (New York: The Free Press of Glencoe, Inc., 1963), p. 33.

A scanning of any list of the most elementary problems common to the new states readily suggests the conclusion that the basic processes of political modernization and national development can be advantageously conceived of as problems in communication. For example, the generally recognized gap between the Westernized, more urbanized leaders and the more tradition-bound, village-based masses, which is the hallmark of transitional societies, represents a flaw in the structure of the national communications and a fundamental problem in personal communications among people with grossly different life experiences.[22]

Restating the national unity argument in the language of communication, we might thus say that political development involves extending central communication networks into and across previously isolated sectors of the society. The developing political system is characterized by new horizontal channels stemming from increased socioeconomic interdependence and new vertical channels arising from increased pressures for political participation and administrative effectiveness. The expanded communication capacity may derive from the improvement of existing national facilities, the penetration and exploitation of existing local facilities, the creation of wholly new facilities at either the national or local level, or some combination of several strategies. In every case, however, political development viewed in this way involves a structural expansion in the communication sector sufficient to make "national" politics possible.[23]

[22] Lucian W. Pye, "Introduction," in Lucian W. Pye, ed., *Communications and Political Development* (Princeton, N.J.: Princeton University Press, 1963), pp. 8-9 and *passim*.

[23] This is what Pye calls the amplifying function of communication whereby "man-sized" acts are transformed into "society-sized" acts. He continues, "To a remarkable degree the difference between private and public affairs is determined by the extent to which acts of individuals are either amplified or ignored by the communications process. Without a network capable of enlarging and magnifying the words and choices of individuals there could be no politics capable of spaning a nation." — *Ibid.*, p. 6.

Much the same thought is contained in Silvert's characterization of changes in the "We-They" feeling as development takes place:

This "in-group" versus "out-group" feeling suffers a fundamental transformation in the process of modernization; even though the sentiment

There is nothing wrong with this view of political development as far as it goes, but as Pye and many others have pointed out it is far from complete. Political development implies not only expanded communication capacity and increased homogenization of political images and identifications, but also the diffusion of particular types of behavior stemming from new ways of viewing self, politics, and the world. As emphasized in the earlier sections on communication and political change, the sociopolitical transformations which may follow on the heels of new communication inputs vary greatly, and all of them are certainly not transformations that we wish to associate with the concept of political development. We can think, therefore, of national integration as a transformation in communication patterns sufficient to support political action of national scope. These changes could then be viewed as a first step or requisite for political development. We are then free to ask more specifically what might be meant by political development in systems which have *already* achieved some degree of national unity as here defined.

Unfortunately, a general communication formulation of political development does not seem within grasp at the present. Such a formulation would have to handle systems as diverse as those of Nigeria, where national integration is a momentous developmental problem, and of Cuba, where national integration is less salient and coordination and control within the newly organized institutional matrix are paramount. Nevertheless, enough has been written about the general topic of politi-

---

persists, its qualitative nature is changed by the inclusion of entire collectivities of persons never to be seen by the individual, never to be conversed with, never to be physically touched. The citizen of the nation-state becomes aware of his fellow-citizens as part of his personal world, sadly or bravely prepared to defend them with his life if need be, willing to depend on their continued performance for the satisfaction of his own needs and at least tacitly knowing that they in turn depend on his continued compliance with a bargain he had nothing to do with making, and of which he may be only most dimly aware. — K. H. Silvert, "The Strategy of the Study of Nationalism" in K. H. Silvert, ed., *Expectant Peoples: Nationalism and Development* (New York: Random House, Inc., 1963); quotation from p. 23.

cal development during the past decade to suggest that some
order can be imposed on the field. In the next few pages, then,
is offered an explication of four dimensions of political development which might be considered *in addition to* the
notion of national integration. There is nothing particularly
original about this formulation, and certainly nothing invio-
lable about its contents.[24] Furthermore, no attempt has been
made to link each of the dimensions developed below to the
discussion of communication that has gone before. The presentation is primarily intended to suggest the types of subjects
with which any forthcoming communication model of political
development will have to deal.

In capsule form, we may say that political development involves (1) increased structural differentiation in the political
system; (2) a movement away from ascription criteria and
toward achievement criteria in political recruitment and evaluation; (3) a widening of the effective scope of political activity;
and (4) increased secularization and "rationalization" in the
performance of political functions. Each of these tendencies
will be examined in turn.

Increased Structural Differentiation in the Political System.
Most simply, this means that, as a political system develops, its
structures become increasingly separate from other structures
in the society and economy. Whereas in the primitive tribe the
activities of religion and politics, for instance, may be fused in
the person of the chief or ruler, in the modern state we expect
to find different and often competing hierarchies attending to
these activities. This fractioning off of political activity is only
a first step in a continuing process of specialization which takes

[24] The explication of political development presented here is a free
adaptation of points made by Joseph LaPalombara in a discussion of political change. See his "Bureaucracy and Political Development: Notes, Queries,
and Dilemmas," in Joseph LaPalombara, ed., *Bureaucracy and Political
Development* (Princeton, N.J.: Princeton University Press, 1963), particularly pp. 39-48. The differences between LaPalombara's formulation and
this one are significant enough, however, so that criticism of the latter
should not be generalized to include the former. The intellectual progeni-
tors of the change and development dialogue would include Weber,
Parsons, Lasswell, and Almond, among others.

place as the system develops. The multiplication of identifiable structures — courts, armed forces, legislatures, councils, committees, agencies, police, and political parties — within the political system itself bears witness to the internal specialization that occurs. *Multifunctionality* in some form persists; that is, the bureaucracy in the more developed system may well contribute to the making of rules as well as to their enforcement, and the courts may contribute to the making of policy as well as the adjudication of differences. Nevertheless the tendency is also toward increasing functional specificity as opposed to the days when the King's minister could at the same time be diplomat, fiscal advisor, knight of the realm, and ornament of the court.

Movement Away from Ascription Criteria and Toward Achievement Criteria. Using the simplest manner of expression, we say that, as a political system develops, people increasingly are recruited for political roles on the basis of demonstrated capacity to handle the job rather than on the basis of birth, family, connections, or graft. A prime corollary is that they are advanced, controlled, and punished on the basis of the same criteria. There is, naturally, always some mixture of ascription and achievement operative in any real system. Our view does not imply any final mix of criteria, only that the ratio of achievement to ascription must be increasing if political development is taking place. Notice that we are not positing equal *opportunity* to achieve, merely increased emphasis on achievement criteria in the selection, reward, and punishment of actors in the system. Also, notice that the ethical issue is muted in another way. The achievement criteria used may well include such specifications as "is experienced in hand-to-hand combat" or "is of unquestioned and unquestioning political loyalty." That a system requires specialists in violence or specialists in obedience is not at this juncture important. What matters is that in a more modern system men are chosen for these roles on the basis of their demonstrated ability to meet the specifications of the job.[25]

[25] Specialists in violence and obedience seem to be among the first to be selected by achievement criteria as a system modernizes. The hired assassins of fifteenth-century Florence, for instance, were recruited according

Widening of the Effective Scope of Political Activity. What
we have in mind here is different from what is at issue when
attention is drawn to the increasing *magnitude* of political
activity which usually accompanies economic development or
authoritarianisms of the right or left. An important type of
political change is indexed by the broadening control of political elites over previously unregulated areas of behavior; but
this does not necessarily signal development from our point of
view. For instance, nationalization of privately held industries
or services implies an increase in magnitude of political activity, but it would go beyond our nonnormative approach to
argue that it also implies political development. Rather, political development involves increased capacity to *effectuate* relevant policy. It is some version of this dimension that is referred
to when political systems that are unable to maintain internal
order, collect taxes, gather statistics, or implement established
policies are characterized as less developed than systems in
which such tasks are successfully accomplished. The capacity
to effectuate policy may well be related to the previous two
points. That is, it may depend on prior structural differentiation and the growth of achievement orientation. However,
since it is not an automatic consequence of changes taking
place along those two dimensions, it is kept separate in this
formulation.

*Secularization and "Rationalization" in the Performance of
Political Functions.* Political development implies increased reliance on the clarification of policy goals and the calculation of
viable ends-means linkages which in turn are based on accurate
knowledge and manipulation of the environment rather than
on magic, religion, dogma, sentiment, or intuition. The extent
to which styles of decision become infused with some mixture
of pragmatism and applied science provides an index of the
system's level of development. Note that the degree to which
the chosen model of rationality is actually approached in practice will always differ from structure to structure, even within

---

to procedures and criteria which seem quite modern even by today's
standards.

the same system. In the United States, for instance, dogma and sentiment have little importance in decision making in the Bureau of the Census and much more importance in the political parties. Even within such less rational structures as the parties, however, one detects movement toward a "scientific" style of decision making in which the latest technology such as the sample survey and the computer are used to explore alternatives and to achieve greater predictability.[26]

The approach to political development just presented should not be thought of as incompatible with the national-unity approach outlined earlier. Both can illuminate the political system in flux, and in fact they touch conceptually at many points. As an example, consider the integrative implications of developmental activity along the dimension of "movement away from ascription criteria and toward achievement criteria

[26] Notice that political development has been characterized as change along these four dimensions in a way that is not tied to normative considerations of what constitutes a "good" or a "bad" political system. La-Palombara makes this point very clearly:

It should be reasonably clear that development along these dimensions can occur irrespective of whether the population participates in the political process, whether one or more political parties exists, whether civil liberties are institutionalized, whether public policy is responsive to the wishes or demands of the people, whether a high degree of political pluralism is present, and so on. . . . A particular combination of attributes along these dimensions might still evolve in either a democratic or a non-democratic framework. In other words, if *democratic* political development is the end in view, it must be analyzed in terms of variables that are additional to those we have been discussing. — Joseph LaPalombara, *Bureaucracy and Political Development* (Princeton, N.J.: Princeton University Press, 1963), p. 47; emphasis in the original.

According to this view, the United States and the Soviet Union (particularly since the death of Stalin) are at somewhat similar levels of political development. Both stand considerably higher on the developmental continuum than such otherwise diverse nations as India, Thailand, Ghana, and Albania.

For an elaboration of this and related points, see the essays in *The Annals*, Vol. 358, March 1965, entire issue devoted to "New Nations: The Problem of Political Development," Karl Von Vorys, ed.

in political recruitment and evaluation." Let us simplify the example by imagining a situation in which pressure for the implementation of achievement norms comes wholly from the political elite rather than from disadvantaged segments of the more general population. Under these circumstances, the reorganization of recruitment practices might involve such things as educational reform; the setting up of special structures to search out, winnow, and evaluate candidates; the use of the mass media and other vertical channels for informational and motivational campaigns of an instrumental nature; and adjustments in the style and level of political discourse in the interests of establishing an elite-mass dialogue of greater continuity. It is clear that we are now dealing with an example of endogenous communication change, an example which would have consequences for national integration going well beyond the more immediate recruitment concerns of the leadership.

In closing, it is well to recall that we have made no attempt to join the discussion of communication to the discussion of political development in a complete and satisfying manner. We do not seem to be ready yet for such an ambitious undertaking. As Lerner has said in speaking of the search for a "comprehensive theoretical understanding of the interaction between communications and political development,"

> No paper achieves such a comprehensive theoretical understanding — a statement of such force as to suffuse us with the beautiful feeling of perfect illumination — as does a Newtonian account of the solar system as a *gravitational* system or a Wienerian account of all systems as *entropic* systems. It may be prudent at this stage of our knowledge about communication systems and social systems to aim at something less than this.[27]

Although no single point of entry into the study of the political system will illuminate its developmental aspects in their entirety, changes in the organization, patterning, use, content,

---

[27] Daniel Lerner, "Toward a Communication Theory of Modernization. A Set of Considerations," in Lucian W. Pye, ed., *Communications and Political Development* (Princeton, N.J.: Princeton University Press, 1963), p. 329. Emphasis in original.

and effects of communication seem particularly sensitive indicators of developmental transformations. Communication changes, therefore, deserve more attention in the analysis of political development than they have heretofore received. Perhaps the "feeling of perfect illumination" will some day follow.

CHAPTER VIII

The Organization and Control
of Communication: Problems
# of Freedom and Restraint

INTRODUCTION

THE political history of Western Europe and the United States contains no more stirring episodes than those which turn on the struggles for "freedom of expression," including freedom of access to information and channels of communication. Certainly the classic Enlightenment and post-Enlightenment rhetoric incorporates a nucleus of ideas which many would still see as perhaps the most fundamental assumptions and commitments supportive of "the democratic way of life." Consider a few of these related themes and their classic articulation:

1. *Man, through the use of reason, is capable of differentiating truth from error.*

> And though all the winds of doctrine were let loose to play upon the earth, so Truth be in the field, we do injuriously by licensing and prohibiting to misdoubt her strength. Let her and Falsehood grapple; who ever knew Truth to be put to the worse, in a free and open encounter?　　　　　　Milton, *Areopagitica*

2. *Freedom of expression for everyone is a basic political right.*

136

If all mankind minus one, were of one opinion, and only one person were of the contrary opinion, mankind would be no more justified in silencing that one person, than he, if he had the power, would be justified in silencing mankind. Mill, *On Liberty*

3. *Freedom of the press is essential to democratic politics.*

No experiment can be more interesting than that we are now trying, and which we trust will end in establishing the fact, that man may be governed by reason and truth. Our first object should therefore be, to leave open to him all the avenues to truth. The most effectual hitherto found, is the freedom of the press. It is therefore the first shut up by those who fear the investigation of their actions.   Thomas Jefferson [1]

4. *Freedom of the press does not include complete freedom from responsibility for the content of materials published.*

The liberty of the press is indeed essential to the nature of a free state, but this consists in laying no previous restraints upon publications, and not in freedom from censure for criminal matter when published. Every free man has an undoubted right to lay what sentiments he pleases before the public; to forbid this, is to destroy the freedom of the press; but if he publishes what is improper, mischievous, or illegal, he must take the consequences of his own temerity.   Blackstone, *Commentaries*

On close inspection, of course, we can take issue with both the normative and the empirical bases of such ideas, as well as with their viability in political practice. For instance, the weight of modern political experience and scientific evidence falls heavily against the Miltonian thesis that when truth and falsehood grapple (whatever that may mean!) truth will tri-

---

[1] As quoted by Fred S. Siebert, "The Libertarian Theory," in Fred S. Siebert, Theodore Peterson, Wilbur Schramm, *Four Theories of the Press* (Urbana, Ill.: University of Illinois Press, 1963), p. 47. The most recent attempts to quantify freedom of the press and relate it to a variety of socioeconomic indices are Raymond B. Nixon, "Freedom in the World's Press: A Fresh Appraisal with New Data," *Journalism Quarterly*, Vol. 42, No. 1, Winter 1965, pp. 3-14, 118-19, and Vincent Farace and Lewis Donohew, "Mass Communication in National Social Systems: A Study of 43 Variables in 115 Countries," *Journalism Quarterly*, Vol. 42, No. 2, Spring 1965, pp. 253-261.

umph in a free and open encounter. Or Mill's notion of freedom of expression as a basic political right has been widely
challenged by both Marxists and a host of others who apply
different values to the assessment of political life. In another
vein, giving meaning to Blackstone's thesis that the state has
the right to punish those who have published what is "improper, mischievous, or illegal" is no small task. As students of
the First Amendment are well aware, in the United States
alone hundreds of court cases and many volumes of discussion
have turned on precisely this point. What is improper, mischievous, or even illegal is by no means self-evident.

However, our purpose here is not to explore the rightness,
coherence, or viability of Enlightenment ideas about freedom
of expression.[2] Rather, we are concerned with introducing and

---

[2] Rightness, coherence, or viability aside, in the American political system, at least, these ideas exhibit remarkable staying power, woven as they
are into the basic constitutional fabric. For instance, in 1951 in his con-
curring opinion in *Dennis v. United States,* Supreme Court Justice Frank-
furter spoke with eloquence as a latter-day son of the Enlightenment:

> Freedom of expression is the well-spring of our civilization — the
> civilization we seek to maintain and further by recognizing the right of
> Congress to put some limitation upon expression. Such are the para-
> doxes of life. For social development of trial and error, the fullest
> possible opportunity for the free play of the human mind is an indis-
> pensable prerequisite. The history of civilization is in considerable
> measure the displacement of error which once held sway as official
> truth by beliefs which in turn have yielded to other truths. Therefore
> the liberty of man to search for truth ought not to be fettered, no mat-
> ter what orthodoxies he may challenge. Liberty of thought soon shriv-
> els without freedom of expression. Nor can truth be pursued in an
> atmosphere hostile to the endeavor or under dangers which are
> hazarded only by heroes. — *Dennis v. U.S.,* 341 U.S. 494 (1951). Quota-
> tion from p. 550.

For the nonspecialist who wishes to pursue "freedom of expression"
controversies with special reference to the United States, the following
books are useful: William Ernest Hocking, *Freedom of the Press* (Chicago:
University of Chicago Press, 1947), and Siebert, Peterson, and Schramm,
op. cit. [1], offer background material. Leonard W. Levy, *Freedom of
Speech and Press in Early American History: Legacy of Suppression* (New
York: Harper & Row, Publishers, 1963) argues against the usually accepted
"libertarian" interpretation of the genesis of the First Amendment. On

analyzing a number of *political problems* which relate to and derive from a focus on such ideas. As the title of this chapter indicates, we wish to translate the debate over freedom of expression into questions about the organization and control of communication. In doing this, we shall interpret the substantive scope of the freedom-of-expression controversy very broadly, as in fact it has traditionally been interpreted by Enlightenment and post-Enlightenment theorists. Thus, as suggested in Chapter III, the organization and control of the rich variety of communication networks which are or might be functionally related to political processes will fall conceptually within the bounds of our discussion.

The freedom of expression issue raises public policy questions of very great breadth and complexity. We cannot hope to do justice to any one of these questions within the confines of a few pages. Nevertheless, by juxtaposing the questions and thinking of them as problems in the organization and control of communication, comparison is facilitated.

THE EDUCATION OF CITIZENS

Over thirty years ago, Charles Merriam reminded us that ". . . every modern state develops a far-reaching program designed to maintain the morale of its constituent members at a point where their activities will fit in with and perform the functional activities necessary for group survival." [3] What Mer-

---

constitutional law and the control of expression, see Zechariah Chafee, Jr., *Free Speech in the United States* (Cambridge: Harvard University Press, 1941) and Edward G. Hudon, *Freedom of Speech and Press in America* (Washington, D.C.: Public Affairs Press, 1962). For a semipopular treatment of the "loyalty" issue as it relates to free speech see Alan Barth, *The Loyalty of Free Men* (New York: Viking Press, Inc., 1951); an extensive scholarly treatment of the loyalty problem can be found in Ralph S. Brown, Jr., *Loyalty and Security* (New Haven: Yale University Press, 1958). Although much outdated, Zechariah Chafee, Jr., *Government and Mass Communications*, Vol. I and Vol. II (Chicago: University of Chicago Press, 1947) remains the standard work on the government-mass media relationship in the United States.

[3] Charles Edward Merriam, *The Making of Citizens* (Chicago: University of Chicago Press, 1931), p. 13.

riam was saying is that all political systems evolve programs to prepare the citizens for participation in political life. All such programs are some mixture of formal and informal, planned and unplanned training, but the ratio varies from system to system. To return to a favorite example, in the American public schools there are aspects both of organized activity (civics courses) and of what might be called unstructured training (confrontation with ethnic minorities in play and in learning situations). On the other hand, in experiences such as the Chinese thought reform, the leadership strives for maximum structuring and predictability in the learning situation through extensive planning and organization of the total process. Over the past half-century, moreover, there has been a movement toward more planning and more organization in the area of citizenship education in systems of the most diverse types. At the end of his review of civic training in Great Britain, France, Germany, Italy, Switzerland, Austria, the Soviet Union, and the United States, Merriam noted that in the modern world (1931) "increasing attention is given to the systematic and conscious development of elaborate mechanisms of civic training, and less reliance is placed upon unorganized drift." [4] The trend is even more pronounced today.

With this trend toward planning, two related aspects of the education of citizens seem increasingly to differentiate systems on the basis of the freedom and restraint controversies which are now our primary concern. Cast in question form, these two aspects are:

Who shall control and coordinate the programs?
What shall be taught and by what methods?

Who Shall Control and Coordinate the Programs? One of the differences frequently pointed out between democratic and authoritarian political systems is that in the former a wide variety of agencies such as the family, the church, the school, clubs and groups, the political parties, and the mass media, all participate in the political training of children and adults.

[4] *Ibid.*, p. 360.

In the authoritarian system, on the other hand, no such plurality of forces is at work.[5] Strictly speaking, this is inaccurate because in the full flowering of authoritarianism the same spectrum of social institutions operates. In fact, the range of institutions important in political education in modern authoritarianism may even be broader, including, for example, organizations such as a people's militia not usually found in other systems. The critical difference, of course, is at the level of coordination and control. In the fully developed authoritarian system the various institutions are linked together at the elite level through interlocking organization, ideological fusion, or both. In the more democratic system there is more pluralism, both of control and content.

From the citizen's point of view, centralization of coordination and control has two major consequences. First, at any one time his civic training experiences tend to be homogeneous and mutually reinforcing. Second, throughout his life cycle, the experiences tend to be narrowly cumulative, with citizenship training activities through school, club, place of work, party, and mass media stacking on top of each other in a coherent and structured way. In the more decentralized system, these tendencies are countered by the pluralism and competition of the institutions concerned. In such less centralized systems, the diversity of points of view represented and the variety of experiences available may not be great when evaluated by the standards of classical liberalism, but when held in opposition to the most centralized systems the differences are crucial. In

---

[5] Although for simplicity we speak throughout of the political training (socialization) of children and adults, in rapidly changing political systems problems arising from planned attempts to *re*socialize citizens are at times equally acute. Young people and adults in many nations now find themselves in political environments very different from the ones in which they grew up. To be integrated into the new system, they may well have to unlearn many of the attitudes and skills acquired earlier. The mechanisms created by the Communist Chinese to bring peripheral intellectuals fully into the system and the institutions built by the Israelis to hasten the absorption of new immigrants into their system bespeak quite different approaches to the issues of freedom and restraint which are raised in all instances of planned political resocialization.

the more decentralized systems, the extent to which political socialization experiences are homogeneous, mutually reinforcing, and cumulative depends much more on what "circles" one travels in and what life choices one makes. As critics of the American system have noted, the progression from middle-class family to middle-class school to middle-class job to middle-class neighborhood to middle-class politics is also a homogeneous, self-reinforcing, and cumulative learning experience. But the seeds of this phenomenon are cultural, not political; and to break out of that particular American pattern is much easier than to break out of the prescribed patterns in systems which attach great importance to centralization of coordination and control.

What Shall Be Taught and by What Methods? Consider selections from two quite different textbooks. The first is from *To Produce, To Save, To Organize,* an arithmetic workbook used in the Cuban Schools for "worker and peasant education."

> . . . in the problems which are presented in the book, we have tried to give scientific information and to raise questions of a socio-economic nature, with special reference to the progress achieved by the socialist countries and, in particular, by Cuba since the Revolution. Also, basing the discussion on numbers, we have endeavored to make the objective conditions that provoked the Cuban Revolution of 1959 stand out: exploitation of workers and peasants, administrative corruption, tyrannical and puppet government, exploitation of our wealth by foreign monopolies, racial discrimination, illiteracy, etc. The object of other problems is to mention the institutions which are growing out of the Revolution, in order to familiarize the students with them, thus encouraging the students' cooperation with the activity of those institutions. Also included are problems which highlight and recall the horrors of war, of special significance at present when imperialism threatens world peace anew.[6]

The second is from *Issues of American Public Policy,* a book of readings designed to be used in the introductory college or university course in political science.

[6] Richard R. Fagen, *Cuba: The Political Content of Adult Education* (Stanford, Calif.: Hoover Institution, 1964), p. 61.

The selections have been chosen with one essential purpose in mind: to provide the basis for extended discussion and argumentation around the important problems which constitute the political dialogue of our democratic society. While no attempt has been made to give "equal time" to every point of view on every subject — this would clearly have been impossible — each section has been organized to raise many of the significant questions in the context of political controversy.[7]

What is there about these selections and the learning patterns that they advocate and represent that relates to our concern with freedom and restraint in public communication? Basically, they raise the complex issue of political "truth," what it is, how it should be arrived at, and how it should be promulgated. These questions are closely related to the centralization-decentralization dimension previously discussed. That is, we expect elites in highly centralized systems to demand unanimity regarding the content of political truth, to claim monopoly or guardianship over its sources, and to promulgate its public version with great attention to detail and the "proper" political lessons to be drawn from these details. Under such systems, a major effort is made to eliminate competing versions of the truth from the learning experiences of the citizen. The distillate of doctrine that remains is elaborated in sufficient detail to guide the citizen into correct political action under all conceivable circumstances. The differences between this and the less centralized system are evident.

THE SCOPE AND LIMITS
OF PARTICIPATION AND DISSENT

In the United States, the First Amendment has come to guarantee a package of what might be called communication rights, rights which structure political participation and dissent. However, as every beginning student of American politics knows, a great many factors impinge on the unfettered exercise of these rights. There are local sociopolitical arrangements which bar many from participation in otherwise well legitimated forms of

[7] John H. Bunzel, ed., *Issues of American Public Policy* (Englewood Cliffs, N.J.: Prentice-Hall, Inc., 1964), p. vii.

expression (Negroes prevented from assembling, speaking, or marching). There are certain occasions on which rights are suspended as not commensurate with dignity, security, or the conflicting rights of others (no picketing at the Presidential inauguration). There are certain organizations which enjoy less than full rights because of special political characteristics imputed to them (the Attorney General's subversive list).

The list could be extended, but enough has been said to suggest that from the American case we could generate a set of questions which also would order other national practices along several dimensions relevant to communication rights. What would such questions look like? At the minimum, they would include the following:

> What is guaranteed in the basic package of communication rights available to the citizenry? What channels are open? What institutions function?

> What topics are not considered fit subject matter for public discussion and advocacy? What are the limits imposed on demands and dissents?

> What groups and strata are denied (by legal or extralegal means) full exercise of these rights? What cultural, political, or socioeconomic variables are operative as discriminatory criteria?

> Under what conditions, by what mechanisms, and for what purposes are the rights of various groups or of the total population suspended or interfered with? (How fragile is the institutionalization of rights?)

If, for a given polity, we could assemble systematic data under these headings we would be well on the way toward an understanding of what type of political system we were dealing with.

Questions of this sort enable us to draw much-needed distinctions between political formats in systems which grosser taxonomies lump together. Eastern Europe is an example. The increasing diversity of political practices within the "bloc" is indexed by very real differences in communication practices. In Yugoslavia, for instance, the package of communication rights available to the citizenry is more inclusive than the package available in East Germany. Institutions such as the Yugoslav workers' councils provide channels through which the masses can articulate demands and express preferences on issues which are not open to debate in some other Eastern European systems. Problems are "aired" in Yugoslavia which in neighboring nations are still not considered fit subjects for public discussion.

Within a given system, the set of questions is useful also for analysis of change over a period of time. The claim of increasing "liberalization" which runs through so much analysis of post-Stalin politics in the Soviet Union is related to changes in communication practices and privileges. Although scholars would probably argue about specific points, there is undoubtedly a wider variety of channels open to a broader spectrum of groups who in turn may discuss more "sensitive" issues today in the Soviet Union than a decade and a half ago. Yet in the strict structural sense, the Soviet political system has not changed dramatically over the past fifteen years. Thus by the study of structural changes alone, much of relevance in recent Soviet political history would be missed. Similarly, the McCarthy era in the United States is not best understood as a time of structural reorganization and change. Rather, it was a time when certain techniques were used to call into question the legitimacy of much of the package of communication rights traditionally thought to be embedded in the "American way." Certain subjects were held to be outside the bounds of public discussion; and failure to express oneself in the new vocabulary of nationalism (or failure to express oneself at all) was taken as a sign of insufficient patriotism.

Although all systems establish some limits on free expression and dissent, it makes a great deal of difference for both inter- and intra-system comparisons just which limits are established, how control is enforced, and which groups are disadvantaged in the advocacy and exercise of public policy positions.[8] In

---

[8] Also, the question of what constitutes proper punishment for "communication" crimes is critical here. In 1663 in England, John Twyn was charged with treason for writing a book in which he exhorted the people to cast off their allegiance to King Charles II and, if necessary, put the

comparative analysis, however, there is yet another variable which must be taken into account. This is what might be called the "environmental" variable, and it enters into almost every discussion of the proper limits of advocacy and dissent.

Consider a key passage from the opinion of Justice Douglas in the Dennis case:

> In days of trouble and confusion, when bread lines were long, when the unemployed walked the streets, when people were starving, the advocates of a short-cut by revolution might have a chance to gain adherents. But today there are no such conditions. The country is not in despair. . . . Some nations less resilient than the United States, where illiteracy is high and where democratic traditions are only budding, might have to take drastic steps and jail these men for merely speaking their creed. But in America they are miserable merchants of unwanted ideas; their wares remain unsold. The fact that their ideas are abhorrent does not make them powerful.[9]

Justice Douglas was arguing that the Communist Party in the United States, by trying to sell its doctrine in a prosperous and highly stable environment, does not pose a "clear and present"

King to death. He was found guilty as charged and his sentence read in part:

> . . . the judgment of the court is, and the court doth award, "that you be led back to the place from whence you came, and from thence to be drawn upon an hurdle to the place of execution; and there you shall be hanged by the neck, and being alive, shall be cut down, and your privy-members shall be cut off, your entrails shall be taken out of your body, and you living, the same to be burnt before your eyes; your head to be cut off, your body to be divided into four quarters and your head and quarters to be disposed of at the pleasure of the king's majesty. And the Lord have mercy upon your soul." — Quoted in Frank Thayer, *Legal Control of the Press* (Brooklyn: Foundation Press, 1962), p. 11.

The sentence reflects not only the state of English justice in the seventeenth century, but also the seriousness with which improper political advocacy was viewed during that period of the monarchy. The punitive measures taken against those who violate the established pattern and content of communication rights continue to be a useful index of political freedom in a system.

9 *Dennis v. U.S.*, 341 U.S. 494 (1951), quotation from pp. 588-89.

danger to the American political system. Explicit in his point of view, though, is the corollary that *were* socioeconomic conditions different and *were* political institutions more fragile, then the judiciary would be well within its rights in prohibiting Communist advocacy.

The problem posed in this way is highly germane to theories of political communication in both the more and the less developed parts of the world. For instance, the many varieties of tutelary arguments heard in the newer nations have at least one common theme: "Our citizens, having limited experience in self-government and only minimal levels of socioeconomic well-being, must be protected from those who would excite and exploit them in order to further private political interests." Central to such arguments is the idea that the class of political "innocents" is rather large and that only state intervention can protect them from those disruptive ideas against which they have no natural immunity.[10] At the national rather than the individual level, the argument is that the tasks of national development are so momentous and the institutions of consensual politics so fragile that only by the sharp curtailment of public debate can the twin challenges of unity and growth be met. As mentioned in Chapter VII, the rule operative under such perceptions of the situation becomes: *There can be no room for difference or division.*

Note that this point of view entails far more than the temporary suspension of communication rights under conditions of crisis or threat. In its most extreme form, it takes the shape of a theory of permanent crisis which argues that freedom of expression is subversive of national survival in the sociopolitical environment in which the newer states must operate.

[10] For a useful collection of writings relevant to theories, past and present, of how and why innocents should be protected by state action, see John McCormick and Mairi MacInnes, eds., *Versions of Censorship* (Chicago: Aldine Publishing Company, 1962). Not all defenses of censorship, of course, are made in the name of the protection of the innocents; the exigencies of secrecy, national unity, and conflicting rights are frequently cited. It is of continuing political interest to note in any given situation which citizens are classified as innocents and from what sorts of experiences and materials the state seeks to protect them.

It would be foolish to dismiss such positions simply as ready rationalizations for authoritarianism, although at times they may be little more. Whatever the motivations of those who promulgate them, the arguments direct us to an analytical problem which is real. Most inclusively, the problem can be stated thus: *Political constraints on communication practices must inevitably be evaluated against some larger background of external and internal challenges to the political system.* At first glance, the problem seems not unlike that faced by economic theorists when they attempt to decide what constitutes "rational" buyer behavior in the face of an environment in which a scarcity of information prevails. In one sense we are asking what constitutes "democratic" elite behavior in the face of an environment in which institutional fragility and consensual scarcity prevail. In each case what is "rational" or "democratic" depends on the milieu in which the actor operates. The analogy, however, should not be pushed too hard lest we lose sight of the fact that the tension between communication rights and political viability contains an irreducible normative component whereas the dilemma in economic theory is only marginally one of ethics. That is, if we pursue the political problem we come eventually to a clash of values of the most basic sort. In a striking passage written two centuries ago, Samuel Johnson stated the dilemma well:

> The danger of . . . unbounded liberty and the danger of bounding it have produced a problem in the science of government, which human understanding seems hitherto unable to solve. If nothing may be published but what civil authority shall have previously approved, power must always be the standard of truth; [yet] if every dreamer of innovations may propagate his projects, there can be no settlement; if every murmur at government may diffuse discontent, there can be no peace; and if every skeptic in theology may teach his follies, there can be no religion.[11]

Both the science of government and the practice of government continue to wrestle with the dilemma today. To paraphrase Dr. Johnson, we can well imagine any number of new

[11] Quoted in Siebert, *op. cit.,* pp. 36-37.

leaders saying, "If every separatist may propagate his projects, there can be no nation; if every critic may speak his mind, there can be no national development; and if every ambitious knave may agitate among the illiterates, there can be no coherent politics." Even the most committed child of the Enlightenment must admit that such arguments deserve careful attention and analysis. Nowhere is the clash between "unbounded liberty and the danger of bounding it" more dramatic than in the less developed parts of the world. And nowhere is it more essential that students of politics come to grips with the intellectual challenge posed by the emergence of this age-old problem in a new sociopolitical context.[12]

THE CONTROL AND USES OF TECHNOLOGY

It has become a commonplace in discussions of politics to pay homage to the changes wrought by the twentieth-century revolution in communication technology.[13] As radio brings news of national life to the hinterlands, as television introduces presidential candidates into millions of homes, and as the "hot line" links the United States to the Soviet Union with a new immediacy and directness, identification processes, political campaign tactics, and strategies of international relations all change. There is no need to belabor or expand the point here. The impact of communication innovations on political life is so massive as to be obvious to almost all.

However, the specific political consequences of the new technologies are the subject of much controversy. Although we can

[12] In his *Public Liberties in the New States* (Chicago: Rand McNally & Co., 1964), David H. Bayley explores these and related issues.

[13] Broadly defined, the revolution in communication technology includes both material and social or organizational innovations. As stressed repeatedly in this essay, institutions such as the Leninist party, the public opinion poll, the Chinese *tatzepao*, and the Cuban Committees for the Defense of the Revolution are all twentieth-century additions to the world's stock of communication technology, but such innovations have been organizational rather than material. For the purposes of this section, however, we shall confine ourselves to the more restrictive definition of the revolution which focuses on the "hardware" aspects of technological change.

agree that the presidential campaign in the age of national television is a phenomenon qualitatively different from the campaign of whistle-stop days, we can nevertheless argue at length on both empirical and normative grounds about why and in what ways the new differs from the old. Similarly, the processes of national integration have been fundamentally affected by the radio, the cinema, and the inexpensive newspaper, but to specify and evaluate the political consequences of the new technologies is by no means easy. Yet even in the absence of agreement regarding their specific consequences, the overriding sociological and political consensus on the importance of the new technologies gives rise to the issue which confronts us here. Basically, the critical question is: *Who shall control the new instruments of communication, and for what purposes shall they be used?* As can readily be seen, this issue takes on heightened political relevance precisely because of a lack of any widespread agreement on just what the new technologies can and should accomplish.

Obviously this is not a new question nor a new problem. It has been with us in recognizable form at least since the seventeenth-century censorship and licensing debates which followed on the heels of the spread of the printing press in Europe and America and which brought political and religious leaders to the realization that the press was bound to be a powerful weapon for those interested in maintaining or challenging the status quo. The issues assume a special urgency and a new relevance in the twentieth century. Among the multitude of factors conditioning this new urgency, at least three should be pointed out.

First, as suggested in Chapter III in the discussion of communication hoaxes, the pervasiveness and potentialities of the new mass media and our dependence on them for political information define a system in which a limited number of persons in key communication roles control vast power for the short-run (and ultimately the long-run) conduct of politics. This point of view was very clearly stated in 1947 by Louis Wirth who, shocked and impressed by the spread of Naziism in Germany, noted that,

> Mass communication is rapidly becoming, if it is not already, the main framework of the web of social life. . . . That they [the Nazis] almost succeeded and that the rest of the world had to pay a terrible price in blood and treasure at the last moment to avert their domination over the world might serve as a warning to those who minimize the importance of mass communication and to remind them that we live in an era when the control over these media constitutes perhaps the most important source of power in the social universe.[14]

Whether or not this political potential is exploited and, if it were, what form the exploitation might take will depend, of course, on the communicators themselves and on the political and social formats under which they operate and in which they are embedded. But the potential is structurally a part of all modern (and even modernizing) mass communication systems.

The second point is related to the first. The scale, complexity, and increasing centralization of the new technology create a host of what might be called problems of access and diversification. No matter how serious or well founded one's "cause" may be, even in a political system which purports to encourage diversity in public communication, it is neither easy nor cheap to get a national hearing unless the organization or individual already enjoys special mass communication privileges or automatic access. As many critics of the mass media in the United States have pointed out, it takes a sizable fortune to found a newspaper or to purchase prime time on television, and the commercial matrix does little to encourage diversity of views on public policy issues. Moreover, the problems of access and diversity are not confined to systems in which the bulk of the new technology is in private rather than public hands. When governments control the media, the basic problems still remain and may in fact become much more acute. Depending on the political format, access to media facilities is still more or less limited to those with money, influence, right ideas, or the blessings of the political elite. In any technologically advanced

[14] Louis Wirth, "Consensus and Mass Communication," reprinted in Wilbur Schramm, ed., *Mass Communications* (Urbana, Ill.: University of Illinois Press, 1960), pp. 561-82; quotation from p. 575.

nation, therefore, if some degree of access and diversity is maintained, it will be because private or public communication elites believe that such should be the case. It is not in the nature of mass media systems automatically to be open to public participation.

Finally, a third set of problems derives from certain technological advances taken both alone and in conjunction with the institutions in which they might become embedded. Whereas the first issue discussed was centralization and the second was access, the third we might call privacy.[15] The most dramatic manifestation of the problem is seen in the new "snooping" devices: wire taps, long-range and miniature microphones and recording machines, and infrared lighting and camera systems. Moreover, such intriguing gadgets are only the less sophisticated first cousins of an electronic generation which includes computer systems for gathering, transmitting, cataloging, storing, and retrieving astronomical amounts of information.

The possible political consequences of such information gathering and processing systems have been dramatized in anti-utopian novels such as *Brave New World* and *1984*. Currently, in publications such as the *Bulletin of the Atomic Scientists,* more serious and informed inquiry into the public consequences of the same phenomena is offered. We need not subscribe to any particular vision of the future to admit that the political issues cast up by the technological advances are very

[15] For the first half of the twentieth century, the emerging law of privacy in the United States as it relates to our concerns was the result of an attempt to formulate some guidelines for what Louis (later Justice) Brandeis had called "the right to be let alone." The focus of attention was on the havoc which "undue" publicity could wreck on individual or group life. This continues to be an important issue, but as argued below it has been complicated by the potentialities of the newer technologies. The problem now is not only one of "being let alone" (not bothered) but also one of *knowing* when you are being let alone and of controlling the use to which information already gathered is put. Although it is not up to date, William F. Swindler, *Problems of Law in Journalism* (New York: The Macmillan Company, 1955), Chapter Eight, offers a useful and nontechnical introduction to "The Evolving Law of Privacy."

real. Already in the United States we have seen administrative, legal, and public discussion on the propriety of wiretapping and intragovernmental use of the records of the Internal Revenue Service. It takes no inordinate stretching of the imagination to realize that the Nazi and Stalinist terror would have differed quantitatively if not qualitatively had the respective tyrannies had at their disposal the full panorama of information gathering and processing systems currently in the design stage. The critical point is that both citizen-government and intragovernment relations may be enduringly affected by advances in information processing. Just as the rapid, centralized, and homogeneous mass media affected and are affecting political processes in ways undreamed of by either post-Enlightenment or Marxist theorists, so the new information processing systems promise to tax existing ideas about the proper boundary line between public and private affairs. The analysis of governmental responses to these new technologies will become a necessary part of the comparative framework within which issues of freedom and restraint are discussed.

CONCLUSION

We have been touching on questions which relate directly to conceptions of "the democratic way of life." Yet no attempt has been made to define democracy or to enter into the continuing debate concerning which of the existing political systems actually is or is not democratic. We shall undertake a brief defense of this strategy.

The rather uncomplicated taxonomic models which classify systems as more or less "democratic," "open," or "free" because they have more or less freedom of speech, more or less political competition, more or less popular participation, or more or less of any other attribute that is supposed to index the degree of democratization, crumble in the face of empirical complexity.[16] The diversity of real systems is poorly handled by such

[16] Out of the multitude of writings on the meanings of freedom and democracy, I have found three quite different books particularly helpful: Christian Bay, *The Structure of Freedom* (Stanford, Calif.: Stanford University Press, 1958); Robert A. Dahl, *A Preface to Democratic Theory*

models, because in both the developed and the emerging nations we find combinations of control, competition, and participation which do not lend themselves easily to classification. The problem is twofold. First, concepts such as political competition and political participation are themselves extremely complex and multidimensional. Second, the taxonomies invariably lack rules for deciding how much of one "democratic" attribute is worth how much of another when neither is present in full measure. The classification problems that arise cannot be brushed aside. The Mexican system is a case in point. There in general are found honest but noncompetitive elections, dominated by a broad-based political party which in turn has partially coopted both the opposition and the public communication system. This combination yields a political format which simply cannot be squeezed into one of the standard classification boxes.

Thus, the previous pages should be read as an attempt to break away from a taxonomic approach to the study of political organization. To mention only two examples, students of economic systems and students of personality systems some time ago passed beyond earlier efforts to construct boxes into which they would sort entire systems. Students of politics are just now beginning to follow suit. It is in this spirit that the organization and control of communication have been examined here. We do not claim that the multidimensional study of freedom-of-expression issues alone is sufficient to capture the core attributes of a political system; the closely related areas of participation and competition deserve careful explication and study also. But as a way into the major issues of freedom and restraint, the communication path is as direct as any.

It follows, then, that we do not wish *a priori* to identify any particular constellation of communication arrangements as "democratic," "open," "free," or their opposites. Our immediate goal has been to formulate questions which, if answered, would encourage the multidimensional comparison of total systems

---

(Chicago: University of Chicago Press, 1956); and Felix E. Oppenheim, *Dimensions of Freedom* (New York: St. Martin's Press, Inc., 1961).

described as ways of organizing political communication. When they deal with the problem at all, taxonomic models usually assume that communication formats hang together in an organic way; that systems allowing little freedom of the press also allow little scope for dissent, few opportunities for public communication up the hierarchy in the decision-making process, and little private latitude in the use of technological facilities. In many instances these assumptions may be correct, but comparative politics can ill afford to leave them unexamined, for the historical record is not that neat, and the future promises to be even messier. As illustrated by the example of the cocoa cutting-out campaign used in Chapter I, the real world of politics forces ethical choices of the most mixed character on both leaders and followers. Series of such choices in varying policy sectors go a long way toward giving a characteristic tone and cast to political life and relations in a given system or subsystem. In political analysis, this intrasystem heterogeneity gives rise to the problem suggested above. In attempting to define the "democratic," the "open," or the "free" set of political communication arrangements, we have difficulty agreeing on how to handle a polity such as the Mexican (or for that matter the American or the Yugoslav) which incorporates a spectrum of practices that does not imply a consistent set of political values. We lack methods for aggregating into a single index communication practices which reflect the political complexities and dilemmas of the post-Enlightenment world.

It is here that empirical theory and normative theory come into most direct contact. As an example, let us pose a classical and continuing communication dilemma. When the consensual bases of political community are less than perfect, how much freedom of expression should be allowed to those who advocate a restructuring of the "rules of the game"? This question cannot be left to the philosophers, for it is part of the very stuff of modern politics. Nor can the uncritical borrowing of the practices of others provide an answer. Few would argue that the resolution of this issue in the United States offers a model which can be made to work without change in other polities. But to express this caution is not to solve the dilemma. As Mr.

Justice Holmes reminded us almost fifty years ago, problems of freedom and restraint in public communication almost inevitably are transformed into problems of "proximity and degree." And as has been amply illustrated, problems of "proximity and degree" are among the most difficult and critical ones for the understanding and practice of humane politics. From this issues a challenge. The quality of thought and research which comparative politics can bring to bear on such problems over the next few decades will be a measure of the maturity both of the discipline and of those who practice it.

Index